Sir,

Published by Times Books

An imprint of HarperCollins Publishers
Westerhill Road, Bishopbriggs
Glasgow G64 2QT

www.harpercollins.co.uk

HarperCollins Publishers
Macken House, 39/40 Mayor Street Upper
Dublin 1, D01 C9W8, Ireland

First published 2024

A catalogue record for this book is available from the British Library.

Thanks and acknowledgements go to Joanne Lovey and Robin Ashton at News Licensing and, in particular, at *The Times*, Ian Brunskill and, at HarperCollins, Harley Griffiths, Marta Kizym, Kevin Robbins and Rachel Weaver.

ISBN 978-0-00-870412-4

10 9 8 7 6 5 4 3 2 1

Printed in the UK using 100% Renewable Electricity at CPI Group (UK) Ltd

If you would like to comment on any aspect of this book, please contact us at the above address or online.
e-mail: times.books@harpercollins.co.uk

www.timesbooks.co.uk

THE TIMES

Sir,

The year in letters

Edited by Andrew Riley

TIMES BOOKS

Contents

Introduction

The question of what it means to be "British" has long vexed sociologists and political scientists, but really it's quite simple: to be British is to have an appreciation of idiosyncrasy and of irreverent humour, a love of the quirky and the absurd, and a broad range of unconnected (and often unconventional) hobbies and hobby-horses. Indeed, the very first letter published in the earliest incarnation of *The Times*, what was then *The Daily Universal Register*, said as much: "One person's affections lie in the price of stocks, and in the arrival of the East and West India fleets; another's in a dreadful battle either by sea or land, in which he can enjoy the carnage, free from danger; a third delights in curious anecdotes; a fourth in scandalous reports; a fifth in horse races and jockeyship; a six in theatrical intelligence; and a seventh in the poet's corner. Thus is a newspaper a magazine or toyshop, where everyone has his hobby-horse."

That letter was published on January 1, 1785, but *Times* readers have not changed – or not much anyway. This volume of letters to *The Times* published over the past year covers everything from playing motorway cricket to the disgraceful lack of grapefruit knives in holiday cottages, the wearing of bearskin caps and unorthodox cures for hiccups.

Humour, which this book with its splendid cartoons by Royston Robertson celebrates, has remained a constant of the Letters page, and since the 1950s the "bottom-right" spot has become the most coveted on the page, an elegant and erudite display of *Times* readers at their most whimsical and droll. It's not easy to write a "funny" or quirky letter, and those readers who try too hard rarely succeed. A bottom-right letter is often unintentionally funny, or simply comes naturally. One thing that almost all of the best letters share, though, is brevity. Philip Howard, in his marvellous book *We Thundered Out: 200 Years of The Times 1785–1985*, correctly notes: "The most common reason for the rejection of a letter for publication is overwriting."

The competition is intense, and even more so for the bottom-right slot. We receive hundreds of letters a day, of which only 15 to 20 are published in each edition. Reading them all is a daunting task but also a great pleasure: *Times* readers are unsurpassed in their expertise and experience as well as in their eloquence and wit. It is rather like sitting down at a dinner table with 500 of the most entertaining guests you can imagine. And on that score, some readers clearly do write at the breakfast table and again after lunch and dinner – or is that supper, or even tea? (Thereby hangs a previous correspondence.)

Whether correspondents write sporadically or every mealtime, I am grateful to you all, for without the perspiration of your brow this compilation of letters would not exist.

Andrew Riley Letters editor, *The Times*, London SE1

Modern manners

Secret signals

Sir, With regard to Esther Walker's account of being kicked under the table by her husband, who was coping with a bore ("Married couples have secret signals. Here's ours", *Times2*, May 11), I made a disastrous mistake and bought a glass dining table. Turns out that even if you are chewing and/or talking, you can still see what is going on under the plates.

Jane Stanford London SW13

Table footsie

Sir, Jane Stanford says she made a "disastrous mistake" when she bought a glass dining table ("Secret signals", letter, May 12). The solution is simple and inexpensive: she need only buy a tablecloth.

John McGuinness Tyn-y-Groes, Conwy

Short, sharp shock

Sir, My wife and I have a secret signal when she judges that I am going over the top at the dinner table (letter, May 13). If I am within reach, I get the kick under the table and a stern look with the accompanying remark "Darling – LLIC". This stands for "long lecture in car". As she is, in fact, a judge, this is best avoided. Until the next time.

Anthony Donne KC Tavistock, Devon

Secret service

Sir, My signal (letter, May 15) to my French partner, when he was over the top, was to say: "OK, Sean." And he would know to shut up because the French for bullshit is *connerie*.

Jenny Ray London N10

Celebrity signal

Sir, My otherwise very amiable husband can, to say the least, sometimes be over-garrulous when he's had a few. My secret signal (letters, May 15 & 16), is to shout "Oliver Reed". He knows he either shuts up or we go home. And he will be walking.

Sue Hudson Kirkby in Ashfield, Notts

Amen to that

Sir, The wife of a clergyman I knew, when she considered that he had preached long enough, would drop her prayer book on to the church floor (letters, May 15–17). At this sign, he – even if in the middle of a sentence – would exclaim "Amen" and immediately leave the pulpit. I was present on several occasions when this happened.

The Rev Sandra Lloyd Freshwater, Isle of Wight

Smooth operator

Sir, Years ago my husband and I became friends with a Spanish couple, Pedro and Loli, who lived in a village where we have a holiday home. My signal to my husband (letters, May 15–18) was to put my hand on his arm and, surreptitiously, gently pull the hairs there. I only realised my gentle curbing of his excesses had not gone unnoticed when Pedro and Loli presented my husband with a birthday present of a waxing kit.

Pamela Horner Sunbury-on-Thames, Surrey

Doting doesband

Sir, I recognised Harriet Walker's description of a "doesband" ("He does it – without being asked", *Times2*, May 11). I have one too. Our freezers are full of home-cooked meals that put an alternative slant on a "ready meal". I am recovering from a broken shoulder and am being waited on hand and foot. Stuart is at present frowning at a muddy rug, courtesy of our young Airedale, who gets a daily five-mile walk. So, not so rare, but I wouldn't let him near a paintbrush.

Philomena Proud Leicester

Sir, I've been a "doesband" for the best part of 30 years. Indeed, this morning, unprompted, I have done the shopping, washing and ironing. However, when I look at my son's "floordrobes", I wonder whether it may be a tendency that skips a generation.

Tim Kerin London E7

First impressions

Sir, Matthew Parris is right that you should never leap to judgment about people (Notebook, May 24). Some years ago, after a dip in one of the Hampstead ponds, I was standing, in a state of undress, in the men's changing area when a group of punks swaggered in. The most alarming – Mohican haircut, tattoos, piercings, leathers, chains – strode towards me. He stopped and asked, rather nervously: "Is it very cold in?"

John Goldsmith London NW3

Ever-ready radio

Sir, Amanda Lunt (letter, May 23) finds it impractical to carry tech around the house to listen to podcasts. I put my phone in a jeans pocket and if wearing a dress or skirt, I tuck it in my bra. I'm never without Times Radio or an entertaining podcast.

Katharine Hersee Great Missenden, Bucks

Wired for sound

Sir, I second Katharine Hersee's place of phone storage (letter, May 25), which ensures I never miss a call. The phone's security is also assured: it would be a brave thief who tried to steal it from my bra. Admittedly it causes some surprise on the bus when the *Ride of the Valkyries* ringtone trumpets forth from my chest, and my outline is a little angular, but the convenience is undeniable, as I also keep my bus pass tucked in the case.

Juliet Barclay London SE15

Code of honour

Sir, Clive McGavin (letter, May 25) refers to the discreet notice in a London club asking gentlemen fitted with a rose to lift the seat. I believe it was Jonathan Miller who posed the question in *Beyond the Fringe* as to the meaning of the (less than discreet) and unpunctuated notice in the lavatories on British Railway trains stating: "Gentlemen lift the seat." He wondered whether it meant that lifting the seat was part of the description of a gentleman, or if interpreted as "Gentlemen, lift the seat!" was it a call for a loyal toast, a military command or even an invitation to commit upper-class larceny?

Andrew Francis Barrister, Serle Court, London WC2

Suits you, sir

Sir, Matthew Parris's Notebook (Jun 28) reminded me of the time I left Moss Bros in Covent Garden with his suit trousers. We had both been buying suits and I inadvertently left with his, and he with mine. I sat at my desk in chambers (I was then a pupil barrister) for some time before I realised my mistake: it was not my handkerchief. Happily our trousers found their respective homes ere too long.

His Honour Judge Richard Scarratt Canterbury

Trading places

Sir, Two of us made the same mistake as Matthew Parris and His Honour Judge Richard Scarratt (letter, Jun 29), but the consequences were more severe: the trousers I had were too long so I cut six inches off. The other miscreant went to his function with trousers five inches above his shoes.

John Chelsom Beckenham, Kent

Innocents abroad

Sir, Mick Hodgkin's item on synonyms for women (Feedback, Jul 22) reminded me of the time my Canadian relatives came to visit and were very confused when we said we were spending a day on the Broads. They enjoyed the trip on the river.

Eva Gordon-Creed Norwich

Innocence of youth

Sir, Further to the letter "Innocents abroad" (Jul 24), I asked my Canadian granddaughter twins, who are just starting kindergarten, whether they had pegs with their names above. Their response was: "No, Granny, we don't have pegs, we have hookers."

Patricia Spellman Thaxted, Essex

Perfect passenger

Sir, With regard to the TMS article (Aug 15) about famous fellow passengers on aeroplanes, I once took my seat in Hong Kong to go to London to find that I was sitting next to Spike Milligan. I said hello, and so did he. Eleven hours later when we got to London, I said goodbye, and so did he. No other words passed between us. What a wonderful travelling companion.

Charles Pointon-Taylor Penn, Bucks

Supporting actor

Sir, On a BA flight from London to Edinburgh in the mid-1970s I was conscious of various air attendants coming to say hello to the woman beside me, who was trying to read her book, *Actors on Acting*. I also noticed the headscarf over jumbo rollers and the vast quantity of hand luggage she seemed to have. As the plane began its descent, she disappeared into the cockpit, only to return once we had landed. And it was then I realised it was Vanessa Redgrave, whom the pilot had invited up to "sit in on the landing", as she explained to me in that lovely way she has of speaking. I remain to this day, 51 years later, schoolgirlishly thrilled to have had my offer of assistance with her luggage (all mine being in the hold) accepted with the utmost of grace, the friendly crew having found more pressing tasks to attend to.

Gilly Hendry Gullane, East Lothian

Superstar travel

Sir, Back in the day I used to be a frequent flier to Miami, and invariably there would be a celebrity on board (letters, Aug 17 & 18). Somehow, while passing the time of day with George Michael, I was inadvertently mistaken for part of his entourage and swept through the VIP sections like some kind of superstar. He was so gallant and said nothing. Travel has never been quite the same since.

Heather Tanner Earl Soham, Suffolk

Game of two halves

Sir, Further to your report "Don't engage with public proposals" (Sep 4), at a football match in Brighton that I attended some years ago the half-time announcer brought on to the pitch a young couple. The gentleman duly proposed to his girlfriend, who accepted. Twenty-five thousand fans then chanted: "You don't know what you're doing."

Matthew Hudson Garelochhead, Argyll

Vape shape

Sir, My ten-year-old grandson was impressed (or possibly horrified) when he caught sight of a vape in my bag. It turned out to be my lipstick in its shiny purple case. I then had to explain what a lipstick is.

Val Oldrey Haxton, Wilts

Look and feel good

Sir, Trinny Woodall's tips for ageless beauty in *Times2* (Sep 13) made me smile: I envisaged hundreds, even thousands, of women (and men) worldwide massaging their earlobes to get the lymphatic system working. Two minutes is a long time – I gave up after 20 seconds.

Carol Symons, London NW8

Banging on

Sir, You write that the Princess of Wales is wearing "curtain bangs" ("Princess turns heads with 'mermaid' cut", Sep 13). Whatever happened to the fringe? I think it should be curtains for bangs in this country, though the US is welcome to continue to bang on about bangs.

Judy Graham London NW7

Lines of duty

Sir, Janice Turner is right to make her to-do list on paper, old-school style (Notebook, Sep 14). But I think she will find it even more satisfying to highlight the item when she has completed the task, rather than running a pen through it. The line-scored-through approach can have negative connotations whereas the highlighted line reeks of positivity.

Cary Labdon Enfield, Middx

Sir, Much more satisfying than Cary Labdon's list technique (letter, Sep 15) is to write lists in pencil, then erase the completed task, watching the list slowly disappear.

Mary Hoyle, Stamford, Lincs

Sir, When writing a list, the first item should be "Make a list". Thus, when finished, there is already one task to strike off. Immediate gratification.

David Reece, Brook, Kent

Canine lordship

Sir, In her eighties my mother adopted her own version of canine exceptionalism ("Muzzles needed", Notebook, Sep 14). Faced with a shop displaying a "No dogs" sign, she would tuck her Jack Russell under her arm and march into the shop, declaring: "He's not a dog, he's a handbag!" She seemed to get away with it.

Sally Rose Aberfeldy, Perthshire

Lethal parrot

Sir, The letter about an elderly lady defying the ban on dogs in a shop by declaring her Jack Russell to be a handbag (Sep 16) reminded me of an incident at my Cambridge college in the 1960s. An undergraduate from a family with long ties to the college wished to keep a cockatoo in his rooms but college rules forbade the keeping of pets. The matter was resolved by classifying the bird as a firearm, which under the rules merely required the permission of the Senior Tutor.

Adrian Conrad Croydon

Man with no name

Sir, It was good to read in your leading article ("Sir …", Sep 19) on readers' letters Sir John Betjeman's story of meeting his father-in-law, Sir Philip Chetwode, when Chetwode proposed that his son-in-law should address him not as "Sir Philip" (too formal) or "Philip" (too familiar) but as "Field Marshal". The pay-off line in Jonathan Stedall's TV film *Time with Betjeman* was that Stedall followed up with: "And what did you call him, John?" Whereupon Betjeman rejoined, with amused disdain: "Nothing at all."

Valerie Grove London N6

Posh pilferers

Sir, With regard to middle-class stealing ("Madam, did you pay for that artichoke?", *Times2*, Sep 19), my son accuses me of this if I take the sticks or cubes of sugar that arrive with cups of coffee in France. He refuses to believe they are mine. I insist I have bought them. I would never grab a handful from a sugar bowl on a table. Similarly, people who "confess" to stealing the toiletries from hotels seem to forget they are included in the price of the room.

Sue Pheasey Amberley, W Sussex

Slippery customers

Sir, Sue Pheasey (letter, Sep 20) writes that it is acceptable for guests to take hotel toiletries from bedrooms because they are included in the price. That is the case for the small disposable bottles, which are now being phased out by many businesses for ethical reasons. However, wrenching large bottles of refillable Molton Brown products off the bathroom walls is simply stealing. When confronted with the warning of an impending credit-card charge, the usual reaction is one of affront and denial.

Carolyn Armstrong Director, Headland Hotel, Newquay

Fond farewells

Sir, I was bewildered to read that a wake was held after the funeral of Michael Parkinson ("Parkinson laid to rest with Barnsley football scarf", Sep 15). That was a reception. A wake is a gathering of family and friends, held around the open coffin before the funeral or cremation, to keep watch and honour the dead.

Gerard Lynch Woburn Sands, Bucks

Wakeful vigil

Sir, Gerard Lynch is right (letter, Sep 18). A wake is the custom of spending the time between death and the funeral with the departed one; in Ireland burial took place within 48 hours. There is a wonderful tableau of this in the Doagh Famine Village Museum in Co Donegal: the dead man lies in his bed in a darkened room, mirrors covered, with relatives and villagers kneeling in prayer. A string tied to a toe on the corpse is connected to a bell, to alert those around him should he wake from his deathbed.

Jo Burden Marlow, Bucks

Model funeral

Sir, My old boss specified for his funeral the hire of a beautiful model, in black glasses and black wide-brimmed hat, to attend his service sitting aside and alone so that mourners would think he had a glamorous mistress. She came and everyone did. His wife and family had known beforehand about this jape, which was intended to shock and impress old work colleagues who did not know him well. It succeeded.

Mike Brooks Sutton Coldfield, West Midlands

Bring back Beryl

Sir, Martin Samuel's Notebook (Sep 22) on his name reminded me of the time, some years ago, when I was at an Alan Bennett book signing: I commented, when asked my name, that there weren't many of us left. Mr Bennett replied in his inimitable way: "Oh, I don't know, it might make a comeback." It hasn't so far.

Beryl Whyatt Welwyn Garden City

Inspiring Bennett

Sir, Further to Beryl Whyatt's interaction with Alan Bennett (letter, Sep 23), I am reminded of having drinks with Alan and some other crew members in the lounge bar of the Midland Hotel in Morecambe after a day's filming. We were reminiscing, having both been brought up in postwar Leeds, when he asked me what my surname was. "Oh, that's interesting," he said while writing in the notebook that he always carried. "Do you mind if I use it?" "Of course not," I replied. I was amused to see, some time later, that Patricia Routledge's rather seedy chiropodist in *Talking Heads* was a Mr Dunderdale.

Martin Dunderdale Tong, W Yorks

What's in a name?

Sir, The baptismal register is a good guide to popularity, and with more than 1,000 baptisms under my belt I have never called out Beryl, Colin or Brian over the font (letters, Sep 23 & 25). Thomas, Benjamin and Olivia recur again and again. Noting my distress, our children said when they had sons, Brian would be used for at least one. What has happened? They have all had daughters. All I can say is: "How long, O Lord?"

Canon Brian Stevenson West Peckham, Kent

Inept muggers

Sir, To further confound muggers Giles Coren may wish to change his phone (Notebook, Oct 17). Recently, a friend of mine was using her ageing smartphone in London when a youth jumped off the back of a moped and snatched it. He took one look at her battered handset and threw it to the ground in disgust and sped away. She picked it up intact and continued her conversation with her sister, who was puzzled by sudden noises and the short lapse in their conversation.

Lynne Booth Bristol

Supermarket suit

Sir, I read Max Hastings's comment about his redundant tie drawer (Notebook, Oct 13) with some amusement. After sitting in court one Friday, I was asked by my wife to call in at the supermarket on my way home. As I surveyed the smoked salmon options, attired appropriately in formal suit and tie, a lady came up to me and demanded to know in which aisle were the yoghurts and why had they been moved.

Chris Gebbie Ringmer, E Sussex

Suited and booted

Sir, Further to Chris Gebbie's letter (Oct 19) about being mistaken for staff at a supermarket, I attended a court recently wearing a formal suit and tie for a regrettable summons for speeding. I was surprised that on arrival I was ushered towards the "trainee magistrates' course" and then on departure I was approached by another defendant inquiring whether I might represent them.

Howard Rosen Upton Grey, Hants

Game of two halves

Sir, I can go one better than Howard Rosen on being wrongly identified within the criminal justice system (letter, Oct 20). Many years ago I was on duty as a plainclothes detective in a football crowd watching out for those causing trouble. At half-time I saw a man running through the crowd and, as he crashed into my back and crouched behind me, he said: "Keep still, mate, the police are after me." The gentleman missed the second half.

Hamish Brown Selsey, W Sussex

Dressed for success

Sir, Further to the letters on mistaken identity, I attended a function in London that required me to wear morning dress. Afterwards I arranged to meet a guest in a rather smart restaurant and, on seeing my guest arrive, I got up to greet them just as an American couple walked in. The man kindly slipped a £10 note into my top pocket and asked me to find them a nice table. Of course I obliged.

His Honour Gareth Cowling Alresford, Hants

Sir, Forty years ago I attended the birth of our firstborn. In those days the NHS made sure Dad was fully gowned and masked. The labour was so protracted that I had to nip out to the toilet. Standing beside me, a very nervous fellow father said: "Doctor, I'm worried how my wife will cope with all this." Summoning all my patrician gravitas I reassured him that all would be fine.

Paul Murricane Edinburgh

At your service

Sir, Regarding the subject of mistaken identity, on our wedding day my husband-to-be, smartly dressed in his morning suit, was about to leave the hotel to come to the church when he was approached by two ladies who, assuming he was the hotel manager, asked him for "two coffees please".

Victoria Hawthorn London SW15

Common as muck

Sir, Perhaps I can add one or two items to Nicky Haslam's list of things that might now be deemed "common" ("No grieving, no podcasts, no Aperol spritz – the new rules", *Times2*, Nov 7): finger-wagging; supposedly amusing tea towels produced by people in the Cotswolds; and putting your phone on loudspeaker – any time, anywhere.

Bernard Jennings London SE11

Crystal-clear

Sir, Nicky Haslam regards crystal coffee sugar as "common" (*Times2*, Nov 7; letters, Nov 8). I don't think my great-grandmother, Lady Blythswood, would have agreed. In the 1950s she lived in a Welsh castle and, as a special treat, used to give my brother and me (silver) spoonfuls of coffee sugar crystals from the (silver) sugar bowl brought to her on her coffee tray by her butler. The challenge was to see how many crystals you could pile up on one small coffee spoon.

Joanna Martin Sudbourne, Suffolk

Common touch

Sir, The word "common" (*Times2*, Nov 7; letters, Nov 8 & 9) was on a par with words such as "toilet", "lounge" and "mirror" in Mitford U-speak. The correct word was "vulgar".

Amanda Streatfeild Chiddingstone, Kent

In-flight ordeal

Sir, Further to Matthew Parris's Notebook on obese airline passengers ("Big problem", Nov 8), on a flight home from New York a very large lady came and sat beside me. She brought a triple cheeseburger and can of drink on to the plane with her. She was unable to lower her tray so simply placed them on mine. I didn't use the facilities during the flight as I just couldn't face asking her to get out of her seat.

Beryl Whyatt Welwyn Garden City

Airline seat for two

Sir, Not all fat travellers are selfish (Notebook, Nov 8; letter, Nov 9). On a flight to the Continent a few years ago I was a little alarmed to see that I was to be seated next to an extremely large young man. He immediately put me at my ease by explaining that he always booked two seats because of his size. Not only that, but he made sure to sit right at the back of the plane in case he needed the lavatory, though he didn't drink anything during the journey anyway, just in case. When we landed he stayed in his seat until all the other passengers had disembarked. I told him it had been the most comfortable flight I had ever experienced, and we agreed that, if possible, we would sit together for the return journey.

Judith McCallum Hemel Hempstead, Herts

Pull the other one

Sir, On receiving the same "Mum, I've lost my phone…" message as Edward Lucas ("Tech giants are letting scammers run riot", Dec 4), I replied: "And which son are you?" The scammer instantly pinged back: "Your favourite," which deserved full marks for chutzpah.

Sally Moss Tallon Rotherfield, E Sussex

Falling out of love

Sir, Given that the average cost of a wedding is now about £20,000, the expectation of a "happy ever after" is high ("The moment I knew it was over", *Times2*, Jan 11).

However, a wedding and marriage are very different. In my own marriage (which is a journey without a map, endpoint or signposts), I have learnt two things: first, I am not responsible for my husband's happiness, nor he mine. Second, before criticising one's spouse, check that you are without fault. It seems to have worked after 36 years.

Dr Jane Smillie Cardiff

Sir, Further to your editorial "Love's Labour Lost" (Jan 10), and its subheading "You never close your eyes any more when I do the bins", my wife and I have been together for a good number of years and she has never seemed to notice that the bins miraculously get emptied. Perhaps she always keeps her eyes closed. It's our wedding anniversary tomorrow. I expect her to keep her eyes open.

Stewart Alcock Filey, N Yorks

Marital harmony

Sir, Many years ago, we adopted a phantom lodger called Norman. He is a slightly wayward character and quite forgetful. When the back door is left unlocked by mistake it is always Norman's fault, not mine or my husband's. Who left the light on in the bathroom? Norman, of course. His behaviour makes us laugh and breaks any tension resulting from the event. He has been a welcome and useful addition to our marriage of 58 years, even if, on occasion, he forgets to put the bins out.

Vicky Chapman Everton, Hants

Whodunnit?

Sir, The phantom lodger called Norman (letter, Jan 13) reminded me of NE Jackson, who was one of my contemporaries at school. Whenever a misdemeanour occurred, the culprit was nearly always Jackson, of whom there seemed to be one in every form year other than ours. The schoolmaster would furrow his brow, try to picture which Jackson we were referring to, and then carry on with the lesson.

Miles Holroyd Ascot

Nobody's home

Sir, It was accepted that my husband and I shared a ménage à trois: for 26 years there was him, me and Somebody who was the culprit for all oversights, failures and misdeeds (letters, Jan 13 & 16). Occasionally, Somebody was supplemented by their sibling Nobody. Since my husband's death I find that Somebody has also departed and I am most unfairly now responsible for everything.

Janette King Northiam, E Sussex

Feather report

Sir, African grey parrots are not only prolific cursers, they also have a good line in insults ("Birds parrot each other and turn zoo's air blue", Jan 23). I once arrived at a party of a friend who had a particularly obstreperous African grey – only to be met with a withering look from the parrot and to be told that I was "looking a bit scruffy today". It was all I could do not to go home and change.

Emma Greville Williams Pathhead, Midlothian

Well-to-do parrot

Sir, Not all parrots are rude (letter, Jan 25). My mother's green Amazon parrot came from Harrods, where it had clearly been much admired. As a result it would proudly squawk "Oh, soopah" at passers-by. It took years for this to wear off, and it then developed a new speciality in seagulls and motorbikes.

Nigel Wollen Bishopsteignton, Devon

Plaintive parrot

Sir, My mother owned an African grey parrot and when I was born it learnt to imitate the sound of my crying (letters, Jan 25 & 26). This culminated one day with the neighbours smashing a window to get into our house, thinking my parents had gone out and left me alone.

Jennifer Taylar Romsey, Hants

No looking back

Sir, The Polestar 4 is not the first car without a rear-view mirror ("Look out for the car with no rear window", Jan 31). The architect Frank Lloyd Wright had a Lincoln built with no rear window as he didn't want to see "where I've already been". However, his chauffeur wisely fitted wing mirrors. Interestingly, many of Wright's early houses had in-and-out drives and drive-through garages as early cars had no reverse gears. Poorer folks had to make do with a turntable.

Patrick Hogan Beaconsfield, Bucks

Ploughing ahead

Sir, I was interested to see Patrick Hogan's letter about the Polestar 4 car (Feb 2). He pointed out that early cars had no reverse gear. This also applies to some modern cars I meet driving along narrow Devon lanes.

Peter Moore Marldon, Devon

Sir, Peter Moore (letter, Feb 3) laments the apparent lack of a reverse gear in many of the cars he encounters on narrow lanes. In the holiday season I can understand his frustration. My solution, when faced with a holiday week self-catering for my family of six near Padstow, was to borrow a friend's horse box. Not only did it accommodate all the bags, food, bikes and beach paraphernalia required, but when meeting oncoming traffic everyone was willing to give way, presumably taking us for locals.

Simon Greaves Sandwich, Kent

Sir, After a police career, much of it spent unblocking country lanes in south Devon, I can attest that Peter Moore confirms Green's First Law of Rural Policing: "There is an inverse correlation between the value of a car and the likelihood that it will have a reverse gear."

David Green South Brent, Devon

Sir, When my late mother was in her nineties, she knocked a total of three wing mirrors off her car while manoeuvring through narrow gaps. Using this as evidence, I suggested she gave up driving to avoid further mishaps. To which she replied that no further damage would be caused to her wing mirrors because she now folded them in before setting off.

Dr Ben Timmis Emsworth, Hants

Time bomb

Sir, The reaction to the discovery of an unexploded bomb in Plymouth ("Text alerts warn of a blast from past", Feb 24) showed a very different attitude to risk than was normal in the postwar years. In 1948, I attended a boarding school next to a disused army training ground, where we were allowed to play. On the gate was a notice that said: "Any boy finding live ammunition MUST bring it to the headmaster's study without delay." The notice was removed after someone took in a hand grenade.

Adam Lewis Radlett, Herts

Jumper shaming

Sir, On Saturday I was shocked to read your article "Tory ministers pay zip service to middle-aged style" (Hilary Rose, Mar 16). Until I read it I was a 49-year-old man, very happy with my modest collection of half-zip jumpers. After reading the article, though, I felt I'd been "jumper-shamed" and began to question all my sartorial choices.

Justin Lanzkron London NW4

Sir, I too was a happy 76-year-old man with a decent collection of half-zip jumpers who now also feels "jumper-shamed" (letter, Mar 19). Not only that: while wandering through the men's department of a well-known store I came close to committing another fashion faux pas, namely trying on a padded gilet. Fortunately, fashion sense (my wife's) prevailed.

Chris Tudball Wolston, Warks

Sir, May I apologise to Hilary Rose for wearing a sweater with a zip on *Love Your Weekend* ("Tory ministers pay zip service to middle-aged style", Mar 16; letters, Mar 19 & 20). I had no idea that such things were "egregious". The manufacturers make no mention of this on the label: it merely says "handwash only". Mind you, as I'm 75 in just over a month's time, I'm rather pleased to be dressing young for my age.

Alan Titchmarsh Alton, Hants

Cardie man

Sir, Further to your article "Yes! Real men wear cardies" (*Times2*, Mar 20), the cardigan my wife knitted me in 1978 (think *Starsky & Hutch*) is still in perfect condition. Despite my sons referring to it as my Wally Warmer, it saves me a fortune in heating bills.

The Rev Ron Wood Galhampton, Somerset

Sir, My husband was given a wonderful *Starsky & Hutch* cardigan (letter, May 21) as a best man present. It lasted for years until moths turned it into a woolly colander, whereupon it was recycled into the dog's basket.

Thesca Pointon-Taylor Penn, Bucks

Imperialist trousers

Sir, North Korea's censorship of Alan Titchmarsh's "imperialist" trousers on state TV and your editorial "The Wrong Trousers" (Mar 27) remind me of a visit to Albania in 1976. Travelling on the one permitted flight per week for western tourists, we were paraded before a stern immigration official. I was first ordered to the airport shop to exchange my decadent flared jeans for a pair of approved Chinese worker's trousers. I then failed the long hair test, so was sent to the airport barber for a short back and sides. Full marks to the Albanians now, though. On a recent visit to Tirana I was surprised but delighted to see that same barber's chair on display in the national museum as an example of the bad old days. At least one regime has changed for the better.

Nigel Peters Chinnor, Oxon

Sir, Having fallen foul of the sartorial requirements of North Korea by wearing denim jeans, I feel that the only option left to me is to wear a Harris Tweed suit and a bowler hat.

Alan Titchmarsh Alton, Hants

Monty Don's jacket

Sir, The work jacket beloved of Monty Don ("C'est chic, c'est Monty! Get a chore jacket like his!", *Times2*, Apr 3) was worn by many agricultural workers in Scotland, where it was known as a carseckie and made from a strong blue cotton twill. Weavers in Fife wore it like a waistcoat with sleeves but my father, a hill shepherd, wore a more conventional jacket style that could be buttoned to the neck in bad weather. His pockets were full of string and nails, salve and penknife plus his pipe and tobacco, and by the end of summer the jacket was much patched and darned where his pipe had burnt holes. A new jacket was bought every year from a draper in Auchterarder and arrived not by post but in their van, which took a range of clothes and haberdashery to outlying farms and villages in Perthshire. The van has long gone, but I expect there are still carseckies lurking on pegs in some farmyard sheds.

Veronica Morriss Newton Abbot, Devon

Dormant design

Sir, I had to smile when I read Hannah Rogers's piece about wearing a nightie as a dress (*Times2*, Apr 15). In the 1960s we did this frequently: I recall going to a ball wearing my very pretty Regency-style nightie and friends who bought white nighties wore them as a wedding dress. Once again, fashion is going full circle.

Stephanie Matthews Ringwood, Hants

Dress to impress

Sir, Stephanie Matthews remembers wearing a pretty nightie to a ball in the 1960s (letter, Apr 16). We were resourceful in the 1970s too. When faced with the prospect of a ball in an unheated marquee on a very cold summer evening, I wore a pair of woollen long johns (borrowed from my father) under my fashionably strapless – but full-skirted – evening dress.

Caroline Tayler Nutley, E Sussex

And so to bed

Sir, In retirement my husband was invited to dinner at high table at an Oxford college and I volunteered my chauffeuring services so that he could enjoy the fine wines. When I showed up to collect him, the college porter relayed an invitation from the master's wife that I should join her for coffee in her private sitting room. Refusal was not an option so in I went, dressed in plaid pyjamas, bathed and ready for bed (letters, Apr 16 & 17). Neither she nor I referred to my apparel and I have often wondered if she even noticed.

Rosemary Morton Jack Oddington, Oxon

Sir, In my twenties (I am now 84) I went to a gala at Drury Lane. The Queen Mother was in the royal box; the diamonds in her tiara flashed round the theatre. I wore a fitted, long dressing gown in black and gold from Fenwick and felt like a million dollars.

Angela Mynors London W5

Arts
and
culture

Pitching peanuts

Sir, I read with delight Giles Coren's enjoyment of Damon Runyon's stories and how his father, like mine, read them to him (Notebook, Jun 6). The reference to theatre security staff searching his wife's handbag for nuts put me in mind of the Runyon story set at a baseball game, where bets are laid as to who can throw a peanut the furthest. The winner, it transpires, has been using a lead blob disguised as a peanut. Security beware.

Julian Barran Bath

Sir, Years ago at Blundell's School in Tiverton my maths teacher, AB Thomas, kept a copy of *Guys and Dolls* by Damon Runyon in his desk. If we behaved, and covered what he wanted us to cover in good time, he would read us the next instalment at the end of the class. Of course we kept our heads down, treated him with the respect he deserved and looked forward to our lessons with him.

Matthew Lewis Cotford St Luke, Somerset

Dress to impress

Sir, Theatre visits seem to involve queues of women being searched (Giles Coren, Jun 6) whereas men breeze through. I have found a simple solution: I ditch the handbag and wear my Barbour flyweight, as the security staff don't search pockets. I am able to pack in at least a handbag's worth of stuff.

Lesley Shanks Woking, Surrey

Bond on my mind

Sir, I had the pleasure of interviewing John McLusky ("Bond cartoons caught Connery's eye", Jun 14) in 1983 for *Amalgam*, the fanzine that I then co-edited. In taking me through his career and how he came to work on the Bond newspaper strips, John explained that he had initially based the look of 007 on the actor and singer Hoagy Carmichael.

Rob Kirby Hitchin, Herts

Trigger warnings

Sir, Further to your report "The hills are alive with trigger warnings (Jul 5; letter, Jul 6), there is a fundamental failure to grasp what the theatre is: not a model for behaviour but a crucible in which we look at what it is to be human. Not a pulpit, but a gymnasium of the imagination. It is, precisely, and by definition, a safe space because it is perfectly clear that what happens on the stage is performed by actors, on a set, very visibly lit by artificial light, and that the whole thing is an act of imagination. Hamlet will not die but get up to take a curtain call; likewise, Falstaff will not succumb to diabetes but will take the padding off.

Simon Callow London N8

Sir, In the mid-1950s I attended a Catholic girls' school. As a treat before breaking up for Christmas we were shown the film *A Christmas Carol* starring Alastair Sim. The projectionist was a diminutive, gentle nun called Sister Mary Rosa. At one point she paused the film, turned to us and said: "Girls, when I restart the film there will be some ghosts on the screen, but don't get into a blue funk, it is only trick photography." The film continued, no one fainted.

Patricia Milner Leyburn, Wensleydale

No laughing matter

Sir, Further to Patricia Milner's letter (Jul 7), my boarding school's pre-Christmas treat was also a film. The warden, an authoritative cleric, stood before some 400 young males and bade us to suppress any thoughts of a sexual nature that might arise during the film – the Ealing comedy *Kind Hearts and Coronets*.

Karl Bailey Tingewick, Bucks

Out, damned spot!

Sir, There were no trigger warnings (letters, Jul 6, 7 & 10) on a school outing to see *Macbeth* at the Roundhouse, London, in the 1960s. At the end of the play Macbeth's severed head was thrust on to a spike and blood gushed out. I thought it was thrilling. I hope none of my classmates was traumatised. Our teacher certainly never offered any counselling.

Amanda Gotham Cambridge

Silent movie sequel

Sir, Giles Coren (Notebook, Jul 4) highlights the challenges of noisy young cinema audiences. Some years ago I managed to get my daughter's birthday party of very vocal ten-year-olds into our local cinema, only to be confronted by an attendant who asked their age. I realised that it was a Cert 12 film. Quick as a flash, one bright spark said: "But we were premature." The attendant acknowledged a scoreless draw and ushered them in on strict condition of total silence.

Ian Elliott Belfast

Vintage tennis

Sir, I have noticed some tennis players are restringing their rackets daily ("Hand Djokovic a wooden racket to add a touch more tennis finesse", Jul 8). The racket passed down to me from my Aunt "Big" Bertha is of Victorian vintage. It is a Sykes Special, weighing 1lb and has gut stringing 20x29, all in perfect condition. The frame suggests that it was well used. During the Second World War, I recall many children in our road in Wallasey playing rounders with it. In stark contrast to today's throwaway society, this was a racket made to last.

Peter Forshaw Kimbolton, Herefordshire

Forgotten fluency

Sir, Your report about an English woman waking up with an inexplicable Welsh accent (news, Jul 14) reminds me of my chemistry teacher at school in the 1950s who told us that when he awoke after an operation the surgeon addressed him in German. When he responded with a blank look, as he did not know the language, the doctor told him that under the anaesthetic he had been talking in fluent German. The only explanation seemed to be that in his wartime military service he had unconsciously absorbed enough to give him a subliminal appreciation for the language. We never knew whether to believe him or not.

Emeritus Professor Keith Pratt Durham

Check maaate

Sir, Seeing the injunction to say "maaate" (Mayor's anti-sexism campaign, news, Jul 25) spelt out makes me feel I should adopt the speech patterns of Alan Bennett. I once came bumper to bumper with him in a car park, when one of us had clearly arrived in the wrong direction. As he got out of his vehicle he smiled and said gently: "I think we have to paaay and displaaay."

Eden Phillips London E5

Theatre blockheads

Sir, I sympathise with Martin Samuel (Notebook, Jan 28). I am 5ft tall, and it is very rare indeed that I am able to see without the sort of wriggling about that he mentions; the only difference is that I am less likely to cause a problem to the people behind me. However, my husband is 6ft 3½ in and is probably a nuisance to others. On one visit to the Coliseum I was having more than usual difficulties and my husband offered to change seats with me in the interval. As we resettled ourselves we became aware of the sound of seats being raised and lowered behind us, and turned round to see several pairs of people in the seats in direct line with us (going back for quite a few rows) also swapping. Clearly, those who thought that they had a wonderful view over my head were disappointed by our changeover.

Judy Shipstone Maidstone, Kent

Sir, Like Martin Samuel I have had my stage view blocked. I am 5ft 3in and a theatre visit is accompanied by the dread of the tall and the wide blocking my view. It's a gamble, even more so for my mother, who just scrapes 5ft. If the rake in the stalls is not a steep one, why can't taller patrons be limited to booking seats further back?

Dr Sarah Nachshen London NW11

In the line of sight

Sir, Sarah Nachshen's solution to tall people blocking her view at the theatre is to confine them to the rear of the auditorium (letter, Jul 31). This is surely apartheight. Why doesn't she just book the front row instead?

Robert Stein (6ft 0in) Oxted, Surrey

Sir, The solution to taller theatregoers restricting the sight lines for shorter patrons is simple: cushions.

Fiona Rolt Blakesley, Northants

Gaming gods

Sir, Reading James Marriott's Notebook (Aug 14) on gaming reminded me of a holiday in Mykonos with our two sons. We decided to take a trip to Delos to look at the ruins, and I was impressed that the boys (then about 12 and 14) knew that it was the island where Apollo had been born. I complimented them on their obvious concentration in Classical civilisation lessons, and was rewarded with withering looks. *Age of Mythology: Extended Edition* apparently.

Emily Fergus London SW10

Game on

Sir, It is not only teenage boys who gain their classical knowledge from gaming (Notebook, Aug 14; letter, Aug 15). At the end of the Ashmolean Museum's exhibition on Knossos, Crete, a side room allowed an immersive viewing of the reconstruction of the palace of the minotaur from the video game *Assassin's Creed Odyssey*. The highlight of the show.

Anna Brunton Iffley, Oxon

Sir, James Marriott's Notebook brought back memories from a trip to California in 2006 with our sons, 17 and 15. Upon collecting our hire car at Los Angeles airport we drove off and realised that we had no map to guide us. It wasn't a problem though: our elder son knew every road in LA from his hours of playing *Grand Theft Auto* and acted as sat-nav. We never chided him again about his love of the game.

Anneke Berrill London N1

Sparky Parky

Sir, In 2016 my husband and I found ourselves checking into our Cape Town hotel behind Michael Parkinson (obituary, Aug 18). When he discovered we were there for the Newlands Test match, not only did he immediately offer us a lift to and from the ground, he also invited us for drinks at the hotel. He could so easily have been a self-absorbed personality but my abiding memory of those few hours in his company is of a man who was primarily interested in us and our lives. Furthermore, his delightful wife gave me her mobile number, together with an instruction to call should we ever visit their son's pub.

Sophie Warshaw London NW3

Bankrupt Brum

Sir, I was heartened to read your report on Venice charging tourists an entrance fee (Sep 6). Birmingham has more canals than Venice and attracted 45.5 million visitors last year, according to the West Midlands Growth Company. This suggests a simple way to resolve Birmingham city council's financial problems: we should charge each visitor £2 a trip. We have more canals and could charge half the fee that Venice imposes.

Richard Jeffs Edgbaston, Birmingham

Serge's bibliothèque

Sir, I enjoyed James Marriott's piece "Alcoholic, sexually incontinent, rude: oui, I love Serge!" (Sep 18). It would have been much more entertaining had the photograph of the great man's desk been at higher resolution in your online edition. I could have spent a happy hour browsing Gainsbourg's book titles but, when you zoom in, all the titles are pixellated apart from *Le Sexe à l'écran*. Very frustrating.

Peter Fattorini Conistone, N Yorks

Musical class

Sir, The late Bernard Greenhouse, cellist of the Beaux Arts Trio, would book an extra seat for his Stradivarius, the cost then being that of a child, ie half price ("Misery of musicians blocked from taking their instruments on flights", Sep 25). On one occasion an agent at the airport check-in counter inquired: "And how old is your son, Cello, Mr Greenhouse?"

"Two hundred and fifty years," came the reply.

Julian Korn Long Crendon, Bucks

Cello class

Sir, I was once stopped by an airport check-in agent for having a tuning fork in my bag. He asked: "Is it sharp?" and I was pleased to be able to answer: "No – it's bang on!"

Jane Cutler Cellist and director, the DaCapo Music Foundation, St Albans

Safe pair of hands

Sir, Millwall supporters may not throw "mighty fireworks" on to the pitch (Janice Turner, Notebook, Sep 28). However, in 1965 as a teenager I was at Griffin Park watching Brentford play Millwall when the dead shell of a hand grenade was thrown on to the pitch. It was picked up by the Brentford goalkeeper, Chic Brodie, and deposited in the back of the net to be collected and placed in a bucket of sand by a member of the local constabulary with little disruption to the game. How things have changed.

Dr Keith Elliott Cheadle Hulme, Greater Manchester

Problematic books

Sir, You report that academics at Cambridge University are being asked to flag up books that may cause offence ("Cambridge library making list of 'problematic' books", Oct 23). May I respectfully refer them to the Vatican's Index Librorum Prohibitorum, which will need updating but which will be a useful base for any modern attempt to bring back censorship.

Tony Langley Chorley, Lancs

Tango stricture

Sir, While I was pleased to see Jeremy Hunt turn to Argentine tango (as everyone should), I was disappointed to read the TMS diarist (Nov 7) describe tango as "strutting with a rose between the teeth". Let me assure your readers that there has never been a rose, or any flower, in the teeth of a tango dancer. That image is a misplaced myth.

David Thomas UK Argentine Tango Association

Rose-tinted tango

Sir, David Thomas, of the UK Argentine Tango Association, says that "there has never been a rose, or any flower, in the teeth of a tango dancer" (letter, Nov 9). He might like to watch the 1959 film *Some Like It Hot*, where Jack Lemmon, in character as Daphne, does indeed dance the tango – with Joe E Brown's character, Osgood Fielding III – with a rose between her teeth.

Sue Forbes Lincoln

Universal footballer

Sir, Further to the tributes to Sir Bobby Charlton (obituary, Oct 23), in 1966 my friend and I, having just finished university, decided on one final adventure before settling down to work: we would drive to Istanbul via the former Eastern Bloc countries of Yugoslavia, Romania and Bulgaria. There were then few foreign tourists and we were greeted with hostility and suspicion at the border: the crossing in Romania had barbed wire and machine-gun towers. A stony-faced guard demanded our passports, scrutinised them and then retreated to an office.

He eventually returned and handed them back. "English?" he inquired. We tentatively said yes – at which point his whole demeanour changed. He smiled broadly, made a circular motion with his hands, said "Bobby Charlton, yes, yes, wonderful," and cheerfully waved us on our way.

Michael Kriteman London W1

Spell of trouble

Sir, Apostrophes are indeed important ("What's Not To Like?", leading article, Nov 18). The name of my house has one, and for the most part my correspondents use it. I was surprised recently, however, to be asked "How do you spell apostrophe?" when ordering the delivery of an item over the phone. Although something of a pedant, I gave up at that point.

Barry Forrester Ludlow, Shropshire

Sir, St Pauls Street near the cathedral is spelt St Pauls' on one side of the road and St Paul's on the other, but at least the council inserted an apostrophe somewhere.

Stephen Barney Wymeswold, Leics

Herculean effort

Sir, It's not just apostrophes (letters, Jan 20 & 21) that are needed to avoid confusion, hyphens also do an important job. I was once surprised at an airport by the sign: "No passenger carrying vehicles beyond this point."

Hilary Bradt Seaton, Devon

El Tel's magnetism

Sir, Terry Venables's man management extended well beyond football (obituary, Nov 27). I was a newly qualified lawyer when my firm was representing Venables against Alan Sugar. A conference of all Venables's advisers, professional and non-professional, took place at a West End hotel. I had an important point to make but was too intimidated by the roomful of people to interrupt proceedings. Venables somehow noticed me and my hesitation and quietened the room so that the "young man can speak". I said my piece and Venables nodded and thanked me for my contribution. At the end, as we processed out of the room, he made a beeline for me, put his arm round me and squeezed my shoulder. I am 5ft 6in but felt 6ft 5in and would have done anything for him at that point. No wonder his players jumped through hoops for him.

Joseph Holder Edgware, Middx

Art of swearing

Sir, James Marriott always provides a thought-provoking read but it is misleading to refer to calling dandelions "pissabeds" or to Ben Jonson's use of the verb "piss" as improper ("English language was designed for profanity", Dec 14). The noun "piss" is used twice in the Authorised Version of the Bible (1611: 2 Kings 18 v 27, and Isaiah 36 v 12), and the verb "pisseth" repeatedly, without connoting impropriety. Swearing is indeed a linguistic art, consisting of both profanities (English is good here, but not outstanding) and obscenities (like the incomparable gift of the f-word). For further reading, I would recommend Melissa Mohr's *Holy Sh*t: A Brief History of Swearing* (2013).

The Rev Dr Cally Hammond Dean and fellow, Gonville & Caius College, Cambridge

Poetry in swearing

Sir, Apropos of James Marriott's comment that there can be pleasure and poetry in swearing (Dec 14, letter, Dec 15), Jerome K Jerome had this to say in *Idle Thoughts of an Idle Fellow*: "Swearing relieves the feelings – that is what swearing does. I explained this to my aunt on one occasion, but it didn't answer with her. She said I had no business to have such feelings."

Tony Gray Chairman, Jerome K Jerome Society

Mind your Rs

Sir, Bristolians have not only clung to the hard rhotic "R" (report, Dec 18), but have stolen the letter "L" from their neighbours. In south Gloucestershire the nocturnal scourge of field mice is called the "barn ow"; ten miles down the road in Bristol stands the supermarket known locally as "Asdal".

Professor Gareth Williams Rockhampton, Glos

Sir, As someone born and bred in Bristol, I was interested to read your item about the rhotic "R" and the stolen "L". Some years ago a Bristol band leader announced a Latin "Americal" set by saying that the first dance would be a sambal, followed by a rumble and a tangle.

John Cobbett Tenterden, Kent

Sir, My mother, a native Bristolian, employed a cleaning lady who referred to her daughter as "Eval".

Elisabeth Parker-Jervis Cheltenham

Sir, Gareth Williams alludes to the Bristolian habit of adding the letter "L" to words ending in a vowel. The name Bristol is itself a prime example, as it was originally called Bridge Stowe, or the meeting place at the bridge.

George MacDonald Ross Leeds

Sir, Gareth Williams highlights the Bristolian habit of adding the letter "L" to words ending with a vowel. One Christmas in the late 1970s, my work behind the counter of the Bristol Wireless record shop was greatly improved by being asked for a recording of "Handel's Missile".

Andrew Pearson Shilton, Oxon

Sleeping in the theatre

Sir, I enjoyed reading "The big sleep guide" (*Times2*, Jan 2). May we now have some tips on how to keep awake? You'll know what I mean if you've ever spent a fortune on a theatre ticket and fallen asleep in Act 1; started to watch a television programme and fallen asleep just as the murder is being solved; fallen asleep after a ten-minute read or, worse still, after feeling very sleepy at the wheel. Somehow I don't think that reversing your "tiring yourself out" tips is going to work.

Sheila Ormell London SE3

Sir, Further to Sheila Ormell's letter (Jan 4), my biggest disappointment about falling asleep in the theatre is that, having decided that what is on show doesn't merit my attention (all too often these days), I wake up to find that the actors are still droning on and the play hasn't finished.

Benjamin Tobin London E11

Sir, A surefire way of staying awake when drowsiness threatens is to hold a small round Japanese kenzan flower-arranging implement in the palm of your hand. It is studded with pins, and is sufficiently painful to guarantee that you will not nod off. It's also useful for stopping yourself crying at inappropriate times.

Jennifer Galton-Fenzi Littlehempston, Devon

Sir, While reviewing maybe 8,000 plays for *The Times* and others, I discovered that the best way to stay awake during boring ones (letters, Jan 4 & 6), along with jamming a pen into my palm and/or keeping an eyelid raised, was to chew. If you keep chewing, you can't sleep.

Benedict Nightingale London SW6

Sir, I can remember absolutely nothing of *Hedda Gabler* save for the last second. Unlike Benjamin Tobin, when I was awoken by a gunshot I didn't have the problem of "the actors still droning on". That was it, I could go home.

David Sinclair Isington, Hants

Sir, In my youth I had the pleasure of playing the lead part in a four-hour mystery play. After it had finished a member of the audience provided us with a memorable compliment. "It was wonderful," he said, "to be able to fall asleep and find the play was still going on when I woke up."

Mark Grant Wallasey, Merseyside

Sir, Some years ago my husband nodded off during the performance of an opera at the Liverpool Empire Theatre. He was woken by a formidable lady sitting next to him, who elbowed him in the ribs and said: "Young man, these seats are much too expensive to sleep in."

Clare Newton Hampsthwaite, N Yorks

Musical snore

Sir, Years ago I took my father to a Daniel Barenboim concert at St John's Smith Square. During the last movement of the concluding symphony he started to snore loudly. Digging him in the ribs only made things worse because he awoke momentarily with an extra loud snort. At the end of the concert Barenboim politely asked the audience to stay seated to maintain the acoustics while the last movement was played again: "There was a disturbance," he said. The audience enjoyed the unexpected encore, and my father, now fully rested, enjoyed the music he had missed.

Richard Wellesley London SW14

Sir, At one point during a lunchtime recital at St John's Smith Square (letter, Jan 10) in the 1990s I vividly recall the magnificent Slovenian mezzo-soprano Marjana Lipovšek bringing the music-making to an unexpected halt. When her formidable glare remained unnoticed, she commanded: "Will the gentleman there stop reading his newspaper?" Only when he had done so did she permit her pianist to start playing again. She was undeterred by the fact that the recital was being broadcast live on BBC Radio 3.

Stephen Willis Chertsey, Surrey

Sir, Concerning concert interruptions (letters, Jan 10 & 11), I remember a string quartet performance at the Holywell Music Hall in Oxford. The players had entered to loud applause and silence fell in anticipation. Before the first bow had stirred, however, the leading musician announced: "There is a noise in the audience." We all listened but heard nothing. He jumped up and climbed straight to the back row of the highest seat and stood next to an elderly lady. "Please turn it off," he commanded. The embarrassed music lover then reached for her hearing aid, which had been making an almost imperceptible buzz.

Robin Sanderson Oxford

Sir, I attended a performance of *Götterdämmerung* at Bayreuth in 2022 at which some of the audience were ill-mannered enough to boo the soprano Iréne Theorin, who had sung the role of Brünnhilde (letter, Jan 15). She responded by pointing to those responsible for booing and by making a gesture with the middle finger of her right hand. It earned her a round of applause and the booing ceased.

Father Richard Duncan Birmingham

The best weepies

Sir, Kevin Maher neglects *The Railway Children* in his selection of films that will make you cry (Weekend, Jan 13). Anyone who has seen Bobbie (Jenny Agutter) running along the platform towards the slowly revealed figure of her just-released, wrongly imprisoned father (Iain Cuthbertson) and shouting "Daddy! My Daddy!", and not shed a tear, must have a heart of stone.

Michael Johnstone London NW1

Sir, Sceptical over reports that it was a tear-jerker, I went to see *E.T. the Extra-Terrestrial* in 1982. Bolting for the exit the moment the credits came up, I was still too slow to avoid hearing a small boy behind me saying to his friend: "That's the man that kept blubbing all the way through."

Tom Stubbs Surbiton, Surrey

Sir, In 1968, aged 18, I sat in the back row of the Chelsea Curzon Cinema watching *The Cranes Are Flying*. It was my first date with the young man next to me, and I noticed halfway through the film that he had tears running down his cheeks (letters, Jan 16 & 17). I was brought up with six sisters and no brothers, and it was at that moment that I learnt it was OK for men to cry and be emotional when moved. Two years later we were married.

Annabel Ridley Richmond, Surrey

Mortified by mother

Sir, In the early 1970s I went to watch *Love Story* at our local cinema. I was 20. My father was away, so my mother suggested we go together. The last scene in the hospital, where Ali MacGraw and Ryan O'Neal cuddle on the bed as MacGraw's character slowly dies, was too much for both my mum and me and we blubbed uncontrollably (letters, Jan 16–18). I was still wiping my eyes when the lights went up and I saw a number of my friends walking out. It was bad enough that they were all with their girlfriends but they all spotted me with my mother. After all these years, I still have not lived that down.

Keith Robinson Hoylake, Wirral

Creative clutter

Sir, It was reassuring to learn that Eduardo Paolozzi's studio was "floor to ceiling with artistic flotsam and jetsam" ("The brash, flashy Scottish sculptor I can't get enough of", *Times2*, Jan 29). It brought to mind Einstein's wonderful justification for organised chaos: "If a cluttered desk is a sign of a cluttered mind, of what, then, is an empty desk a sign?"

Andrew Copeman London W6

Rugby legend

Sir, I was pleased that your excellent obituary of Barry John (Feb 5) made reference to "the mythical fly-half factory situated deep in the Rhondda Valley". I suspect I was not the only reader to be reminded of the lines of Max Boyce referring to that factory:

"Disaster struck this morning
When a fitter's mate named Ron
Cracked the mould of solid gold
That once made Barry John."

We shall not see his like again.
Alun Evans London SE10

Pike's prognosis

Sir, In your obituary of Ian Lavender (Feb 6) you state that Private Pike "failed his medical for the army because he was allergic to corned beef". In fact Pike wished to join the RAF, and in the *Dad's Army* episode "When You've Got to Go" (September 1975) he failed his medical because of being in a rare blood group. It was Private Walker, played by James Beck, who had an allergy to corned beef and was rejected for military service in "The Loneliness of the Long Distance Walker" (March 1969).

Perhaps I should get out more.

Christopher Westlake Bridgwater, Somerset

Intoxicated English

Sir, Noting that Scots are said to have more than 400 words for snow, my only surprise at the discovery that the English language has 546 drunkonyms was that it seems an underestimate ("English is intoxicated with synonyms", Feb 20). My interest is in more medical or anatomical drunkonyms such as bladdered, pie-eyed or legless. I would also suggest that being trollied nowadays implies waiting for a protracted period in A&E.

Dr David Carvel (ret'd GP) St Andrews, Fife

Early doors

Sir, Susie Goldsbrough thinks retired people like early curtains ("You're already pricing us out of theatre, don't time us out too", Notebook, Feb 26). Not me. We elderly retired people like to eat before, not after, the play. Hence 7.30pm starts are perfect. Dinner at 6pm somewhere nice and quiet, done by 7pm, walk very slowly to the theatre, eventually find the bloody tickets on our phones, time for a trip to the lavatory, and settle into our seats. Just right.

Moira Yip London SW6

Tickets please

Sir, Moira Yip's letter ("Early doors", Feb 29) made me laugh out loud with her reference to "eventually find the bloody tickets on our phones". I am one of many volunteers at East Riding Theatre; I am 71 and awaiting cataract operations, so on "front of house" shifts always prioritise those who have had the temerity to destroy the planet by printing their tickets, rather than the queues of people desperately searching their phones.

Carolyn Booth-Jones Beverley, E Yorks

Naked truth

Sir, With reference to your leading article on World Book Day ("Turning the page", Mar 8), I suggested that my daughter send her son to school dressed as the emperor in *The Emperor's New Clothes*, thus saving time and expense. On reflection we agreed that it was too cold in March.

Anna Terrington London SW4

Minimal costume

Sir, Anna Terrington suggested that her grandson go to school dressed as the emperor in *The Emperor's New Clothes* for World Book Day, but the idea was rejected because of the cold weather (letter, Mar 9). My grandnephew went to school in his swimming trunks as his hero Adam Peaty, the Olympic swimmer and author of *The Gladiator Mindset.* He solved the cold weather issue by carrying his Dryrobe.

Eileen Roddy Northam, Devon

End of local papers

Sir, William Hague encapsulated the plight of the *Birmingham Post* ("Death of local papers threatens democracy", Mar 12). Years ago I stopped to offer a lift into Birmingham to an elderly lady standing at a bus stop. She looked briefly into my car, accepted my offer and I dropped her off in town. The next day a letter appeared in the *Birmingham Post* saying that she had been offered a lift by a gentleman that she did not know, but when she had looked into the car and had seen he had a copy of the *Birmingham Post*, she knew that it was safe to accept.

Anthony Collins Edgbaston, Birmingham

Horrible haitches

Sir, It was satisfying to see mispronunciation given the treatment it deserves ("Humbled Rajan vows to drop those haitches", Apr 9). Alas, Amol Rajan's "haitch" is the tip of the iceberg. The proliferation of elongated "ayes" and "thees" has reached epidemic proportions. For example: "Thee prime minister is chairing ay meeting." The two most common words in the English language have been stretched hopelessly out of shape, initially by reporters and newscasters hoping for a nanosecond to think ahead. Now everyone is piling in: Rajan leads the charge, with Gary Lineker his twin striker.

Tony Francis, ex-BBC presenter, Hawridge, Bucks

Nether regions

Sir, Amol Rajan's haitches and missing "t"s can be irritating (letter, Apr 10) but at least he doesn't lengthen words by inserting extra syllables. A Radio 4 weatherman repeatedly refers to Engerland, Scotterland and the Midderlands. Other radio speakers have mentioned atherletes, arthuritis and diggernity (not at the same time). It's iggernorant.

Joanne Aston Norby, N Yorks

All things trite and beautiful

Sir, We are fortunate in this country to have such a splendid repertoire of hymns: English, Welsh, Anglican, Non-Conformist, mighty, joyous, reflective, peaceful. Why, then, do we have to suffer *All Things Bright and Beautiful*? It is chosen by about half the participants in the weddings I play for (though I am often successful in helping them to choose something better). The hymn was published in 1848 in Mrs Alexander's *Hymns for Little Children*: it should have stayed there. I find the saccharine doggerel, combined with the jingly tune (not that easy for congregations to sing, actually), deeply depressing – especially when there are so many wonderful alternatives.

Lord Lisvane, chairman, Royal College of Organists; clerk of the House of Commons 2011–14

Sir, Lord Lisvane may not like *All Things Bright and Beautiful* but it is one of the few hymns that many people know. Even then, ministers can find themselves singing a solo in front of a silent, non-singing congregation. I do wonder if the default for weddings and funerals where hymns are sung should be a karaoke-style backing track so that the congregation can sing along.

The Rev Peter Crumpler St Albans

Sir, For me, the reason *All Things Bright and Beautiful* remains such a popular hymn is because it sums up everything good about my childhood, especially the first two lines. We sang it regularly right through my school years, it was sung at my wedding and I intend it to be sung at my funeral. Furthermore, I have requested those first two lines be engraved on my headstone, should I be given one.

Wendy Farrington Kendal, Cumbria

Sir, Alas, *All Things Bright and Beautiful* (letters, Apr 30 & May 1) is now almost mandatory at baptisms, not just weddings and funerals. Grasping the nettle, I add sound effects to the accompaniment: little birds tweeting, rivers running by and cold winds blowing, for example. Some find these devices either charming enhancements or cheap embellishments underlining the triteness of this hymn. Job done!

Simon Eadon Organist, St Andrew's Church, Yetminster, Dorset

Sir, Lord Lisvane should be congratulated for his skilful assassination of the achingly dull hymn *All Things Bright and Beautiful*. But I would also beg him to consider adding the insufferable *Lord of the Dance* to his hit list. Too many young ears have been tortured over the years: enough is enough.

The Rev Al Gordon Rector of Hackney, London E8

Sir, I congratulate Lord Lisvane on his success rate persuading couples out of *All Things Bright and Beautiful* at their weddings. I once, after a lot of effort, had a similar success against *I Vow to Thee My Country* (totally inappropriate, if you read the words). I couldn't argue, then, with their replacement choice: *All Things Bright and Beautiful*.

The Rev Annabelle Elletson Crickhowell, Powys

House
and
home

Cat and mouse

Sir, Further to Carol Midgley's cat saga ("I've been savaged by a cat. The pain is intense, the laughter is worse", Jun 7), my husband rescued our panicking kitten from a neighbour's furniture-packed garage, only to suffer similar "gratitude" to Carol's. Arriving at A&E, he was piqued to have nurses laugh at his plight: next in line was a patient with a mouse bite from an unsuccessful trapping.

Irma Ireland Edinburgh

North-south divide

Sir, Further to your report "The true north-south divide? Where Greggs meets Pret", Jun 8), another parameter that Dr Robin Smith might like to investigate to add to his Greggs/Pret and Morrisons/Waitrose indexes is the placing of taps in washbasins and baths. It would be interesting to know if there is a geographical correlation between all three. I have noticed over many decades that roughly north of a line between the Humber and the Bristol Channel, the hot tap is more likely to be installed on the right and the cold tap on the left. South of that line it's the opposite. All mixer taps follow the southern convention, which may mean it will prevail in the long term as such sophisticated innovations proliferate northwards.

Antony Warren Cambridge

Sir, We need to go further back than William the Conqueror for the origins of the Pret/Greggs divide or the Waitrose/Morrisons index. The Fosse Way, built by the Romans in the 1st century, neatly marks the divide between highland and lowland zones: largely pastoral and itinerant to the northwest, agricultural and settled to the southeast. The Exeter to Lincoln line may run a little further north than the Watford Gap but little has changed in 2,000 years.

Dr Anthony Poole Harrogate, N Yorks

Sir, When I lived in Quebec we had an apartment where the bath had been installed by an English-speaking person. The cold tap had a C on it. The hot tap had at some point been replaced by a French Canadian and it also had a C, this time for *chaud*. Confusing.

Imogen Thomas Saffron Walden, Essex

Sharp as a knife

Sir, I know I run the risk of being labelled a pedant, but Carl Elsener did not take out a patent for a "penknife" in 1897 (On this day, Jun 12). The knife in question was a pocket knife.

Mike O'Malley Orpington, Kent

Roman utility tool

Sir, There is a Roman "Swiss Army knife" circa AD 201 to AD 300 in the Fitzwilliam Museum, Cambridge (letter, Jun 13; On this day, Jun 12). As well as a knife it has a three-pronged fork, spoon, spatula, pick and spike, all of which fold up neatly to form a pocket "set" for a Roman soldier.

Linda Taylor Teversham, Cambs

The cheek of it

Sir, Ann Treneman came off lightly on her visit to Portofino ("Rich and tacky", Notebook, Jun 17). Fifteen years ago, when staying in Sorrento, my sister and I visited a public convenience and were charged a euro each. Two small sheets of lavatory paper were offered: one sheet each.

Elaine Laney Cocking, W Sussex

Sour note

Sir, Further to Ann Treneman's Notebook on Portofino ("Rich and tacky", Jun 17; letter, Jun 19), we visited Venice last September and decided to have a drink at a café in St Mark's Square. We knew it would be expensive but were somewhat taken aback to be charged six euros per person for the background music. I still have the bill to prove it.

Jennie Brinsden Rowledge, Surrey

Paying for music

Sir, As a regular visitor to Venice, I must take issue with Jennie Brinsden (letter, Jun 21), who objects to being charged €6 for the "background music" at a café in St Mark's Square. There has been live music at the famous Caffè Florian and its rival Caffè Quadri for hundreds of years. The bands performing are so good that a lot of tourists come and listen to them without eating or drinking at the cafés. They earn their corn.

David Robson Oxford

Cheap at the price

Sir, When we visited Venice in 2014, a small beer, small coffee and a club sandwich on the terrace outside Caffè Florian cost €68, so the charge for the music was academic (letters, Jun 21 & 22).

Edward Baker Tunbridge Wells

Reach for the sky

Sir, When a colleague, the broadcaster Robert Robinson, interviewed Douglas Bader, he picked up the cocky arrogance that Ben Macintyre recounts ("Bader was a hero but he was also a brute", comment, Jun 17). "He may be a hero," Robinson said afterwards, "but after a few minutes you want to shout, 'Race you down the corridor.'"

Will Wyatt Managing director of BBC Television 1991–96, London W6

Boosted by Bader

Sir, In the 1970s I was the hospital secretary at Mile End Hospital in the East End. A young local man had been in a very bad accident, which resulted in him becoming an amputee. Bader visited the hospital specifically to give him support. He was very encouraging: I remember vividly how he threw himself on the floor and picked himself up to show what was possible. I know the patient very much appreciated the visit.

Jamie Sharpley Woking, Surrey

Flying visit

Sir, My experience of Douglas Bader took place 62 years ago when I was in the school's cadet corps. We had had a night exercise and had camped afterwards. Next morning we all changed into our (khaki serge) uniforms and assembled on parade to await the visit of the great man. The time for his arrival came and went and we waited and waited – not a comfortable experience as it was a very warm summer's day. Then, about an hour after the due arrival time, three cars drove on to the makeshift parade ground and Bader alighted. He hardly moved from the car, looked around and said: "Well, boys, it's a hot day and so I will not keep you." He got back in the car and off he went. It was, of course, a privilege to have seen this RAF hero in the flesh but it was more a perspiring than inspiring event.

John Story London SW13

Reach for the story

Sir, In 1966, as a (very) young woman staffer on the *Observer Magazine*, I was sent to interview Douglas Bader at the Royal Dutch Shell building at Waterloo. I was nervous anyway – the man was a legend – and made speechless by his words of greeting: "Famous legless arse, aren't I, m'dear?"

Marcelle Bernstein West Molesey, Surrey

Glorious Bader

Sir, As an eight-year-old boy I nearly died on the Epping New Road when a passenger in Douglas Bader's sports car. As he overtook a lorry with another bearing down on us from the opposite direction, he uttered the words: "On, on – no guts, no glory!"

John O'Sullivan Hursley, Hants

Red-carpet revelry

Sir, The National Trust's "reweave" of the carpet at Saltram (Jun 19) is a triumph of restoration. The curators of the National Trust for Scotland took a similar approach when the chenille carpet in the library at Haddo House was under threat. The copy was so exact that it brought with it a bonus for social historians: a record of family celebrations over more than a century in the form of a number of faithfully reproduced wine stains.

Simon Welfare Aboyne, Aberdeenshire

Welsh welcome

Sir, I laughed out loud at Kevin Maher's description of holiday cottage experiences in Wales (*Times2*, Jun 26). I could relate well to his experiences and could add many more of my own, having rented cottages in Wales every year for decades. Despite the cost of cottages having doubled in the past two or three years, the descriptions and facilities have not improved one iota. I have become adept at looking for information that the website doesn't tell you, such as: parking nearby, toilet roll not provided (yes really, not even one), bring your own towels, overlooks an A-road with lorries thundering past all day, surrounded by neighbours, chop your own logs, and tiny shower cubicle on the landing. Strangely I never find issues with holiday homes in Scotland or Northumberland.

Linda Miller Dereham, Norfolk

Failure to cut it

Sir, I understand the frustration of Kevin Maher (Times 2, Jun 26) and Linda Miller (letter, Jun 27) in finding that their Welsh holiday cottages were not up to expectation. To balance this, I can think of someone who gave my holiday rental property in Pembrokeshire a poor rating on the basis of "no grapefruit knives".

Gary Bullard Richmond, Surrey

Holiday essentials

Sir, Gary Bullard's critical guest at his holiday cottage in Pembrokeshire (letter, Jun 28) would no doubt agree with an entry in the visitors' book at our rural gîte in Charente that concluded: "Reasonably well equipped but no oyster knives."

Dr Allan J Norris Bridport, Dorset

Critical guests

Sir, We let our holiday cottage in Cornwall through a local agency for more than 25 years (letters, Jun 28 & 29). We soon stopped leaving a visitors' book out after someone wrote that there was a bit of peeling wallpaper on the ceiling in the airing cupboard. In recent years the cottage has been used exclusively for family and friends. It has always been very well equipped (we have two grapefruit knives). However, this has not deterred one of our granddaughters, at the age of eight, from complaining that there is no bagel function on the toaster.

Angela Bostock Exeter

Sir, Some years ago, when living in England, I hosted a young French exchange student. Shortly after his arrival, he made the customary call home, and his opening sentence was: "They are very nice, but Maman, they have a tin-opener!"

Dominica Jewell Bazoches au Houlme, France

Grating critics

Sir, I sympathise with Gary Bullard (letter, Jun 28). Our Welsh holiday cottage was slated with a long tirade about the lack of a cheese grater. It was doubly frustrating as there were three to choose from.

Jane Liddy Dodworth, S Yorks

Sir, One of our visitors wrote: "Very small television, but luckily there was a pair of binoculars in the drawer."

Nicholas Robertson Thorpe Malsor, Northants

Grateful guests

Sir, We were amused by your correspondence on the inadequacies of holiday rental cottages. We have a second home with possibly the world's worst carpet and an oven that is nigh impossible to use. Yet we have had extraordinary thanks, have never received a complaint and are still trying to discover which kind guest left us a very smart coffee machine. The secret? We give free holidays to people with cancer via the charity Something To Look Forward To. If anyone is fed up with complaints or would like to use an asset to help others we would recommend such an approach.

Simon and Hannah Blackrock Hawkley, Hants

To have and to hold

Sir, Amy Nuttall's seventh rule – "full access to each other's phones at all times" – has always been rigorously adhered to by my wife, as she will often peruse my phone in the evening ("The 7 rules to save a marriage? I know mine", *Times2*, Jul 5). The only consternation this causes is when she discovers a family invitation or event that I have forgotten to mention, which is primarily why she goes through my phone. And, coincidentally, why I let her.

Ben Wolfin London NW7

Rules of marriage

Sir, Further to Esther Walker's article on the seven rules to save a marriage (*Times2*, Jul 5; letter, Jul 6), in 1981, after the birth of my second son, I wept during my six-week check-up with my GP. He spoke to my husband the next day: "I give your marriage six months. Your wife needs a break from your home. Take her out once a week. Babysitters are cheaper than divorce." We still have a date each week and have just reached our golden wedding anniversary.

Debby Horsman Pavenham, Beds

Sir, Until losing my wife to illness, we spent 53 years of happy marriage together by observing two simple rules: separate bank accounts from the outset and never opening each other's mail.

Pete Taylor Virginia Water, Surrey

Esteemed organs

Sir, Caitlin Moran's article on "the Cobham Road Willies" (Celebrity Watch, Jul 14) described the paint-spraying of male genitalia on our potholed roads as a very English version of the French riots. Unlike the French unrest, which seems endless, I have to report that the majority of the genitalia have been removed but, sadly, most of the potholes remain. More traffic is using local roads than ever imagined and the genitalia were particularly useful at night in warning unsuspecting motorists of impending potholes. Perhaps if Surrey county council merged their graffiti-removal and pothole-repairing departments, then our genitalia would last longer and our potholes would be repaired more quickly.

Sir Gerald Acher Chairman, Cobham Heritage Trust

Troublesome men

Sir, Your splendid columnist Caitlin Moran notes there are no sections for works about men in bookshops in which to place her new bestseller *What About Men?* She also said it was time for men to author their own stories of emotional turmoil rather than leave it up to the sisters. Well, as long ago as 1984, the BBC commissioned me to write exactly such a book to accompany the BBC2 series *The Trouble with Men*. The bookshops? They immediately stuck it in the section headed "Women".

Phillip Hodson Tetbury, Glos

Lion shares

Sir, Part of our family history is the story of a lion in Berlin ("Bedlam as Berlin hunts for lioness on loose", Jul 21). During the Second World War, under nightly bombardment, residents thought it safer to sleep in the park. Our great-great-aunt spent a night on one of the benches, and was joined by someone wearing a thick fur coat. When morning broke she found a lion curled up next to her. The zoo had been bombed and the poor lion sought the only source of security it had ever known, a human. It trotted off without harming her.

Annette Shelford Chailey, E Sussex

Estate of mind

Sir, The end of an era of motoring arrives, with the demise of the Volvo estate (report, Aug 3). Our family's V70, 1999 vintage, quietly rumbles on with 175,000 miles on the clock, offering sofa-like seats, unsurpassed safety with its tank-like construction, and the ability to transport almost anything (an entire dining room suite once) inside its capacious body. It is a reliable and handsome vehicle, and a pleasure to drive, and we will miss it immeasurably when spare parts finally become totally unavailable.

K Lyons Sudbury, Suffolk

Long road ahead

Sir, Keeping older cars running need not be too much of a worry. The owner of the old Volvo (letter, Aug 4) needs to join an owners' group that will advise. We find it is also useful to have a metal turning lathe, handbooks and lots of tools. As a result our old car runs beautifully. Mind you, since she was built in 1933 and has an ash frame we do also have to check occasionally for woodworm.

June and Simon Keeble Storrington, W Sussex

Sir, When I was 60 I visited a Volvo garage. I mentioned to the salesman the Volvo's reputation for not rusting. He eyed me up and down before saying: "Yes, Sir, this will see you out." I bought a Mercedes.

Dr James Beales (aged 99) Henley on Thames, Oxon

Awkward age

Sir, As I sit here – ten months into my fifties – reading about Noel Gallagher's worsening memory ("Right on cue: older Noel forgets his lines", Aug 11), nursing the elbow pain I developed after a light gym session, the backache I got lifting a plant pot out of the car, the mouth ulcer I have after biting my cheek and the ankle sprain I somehow suffered during my sleep, I can only concur with Gallagher's assessment of the health vagaries of one's sixth decade.

Robert Willock Palm Jumeirah, Dubai

Grand old age

Sir, As I get older I find it takes a while for my brain to warm up. Reading Robert Willock's letter (Aug 12), it took me ten whole minutes to realise we are related.

Matthew Willock Maidstone, Kent

Age of infirmity

Sir, Robert Willock (letters, Aug 12 & 14), in his early fifties, can hardly invoke old age as an explanation for his recent ankle problem. The more likely explanation is that he has gout. Episodes frequently start at night and I have lost count of the number of patients who have told me, over the years, how they apparently sprained their ankle or stubbed their big toe while in bed at night. It is also the probable explanation for his recent episodes of elbow and back pain.

Dr Oliver Duke Consultant rheumatologist (ret'd), London SW2

That Sunday feeling

Sir, While I share many of Robert Willock's health vagaries (letter, Aug 12, 14 & 15), my main one is rather harder to identify. I often find a day will "feel" like another day of the week. An example: while purchasing an item at our local chemist I commented that I was surprised to find them open on a Sunday. "That's because it's a Saturday," came the curt reply. I hastily exited the shop but the correction was not enough to change my brain's perception for the remainder of that day.

Carol Coyne Walton-on-Thames, Surrey

Dread of holidays

Sir, Further to James Marriott's holiday angst ("Holidays are the dream – until the dread sets in", Notebook, Aug 22), some years ago I bought an original copy of a newspaper cartoon showing a cleric within a sandcastle pulpit, with his wife and son beneath looking upwards and his wife saying: "I wish your father could learn to relax on holiday." I hope James has better luck.

Sally Lewers Poundbury, Dorset

Trapping bedbugs

Sir, With regard to the menace of bedbugs ("Bedbug infestation getting worse, UK pest firm warns", Oct 12), my wife has reminded me of a scene from the film *A Taste of Honey* in which Paul Danquah shows Rita Tushingham the trick for removing them: taking a moistened bar of soap and patting it down on the bugs as they move on the sheet. The bugs stuck to the soap.

Vyvyan Hardless Bembridge, Isle of Wight

Sir, I don't think a bar of wet soap would solve a bedbug problem (letter, Oct 14). It was Leslie Caron in *The L-Shaped Room*, not Rita Tushingham in *A Taste of Honey*, who was advised to collect bedbugs on a bar of soap, not to get rid of them but to present them to the landlady as irrefutable evidence of their existence.

Michael Longman Bristol

Test tube

Sir, There may be many London Underground stations, but only two names contain all the vowels: Ealing South and Mansion House ("Underground Movement", leading article, Nov 6). This is my favourite quiz question.

Alan Hadfield Maidstone, Kent

Mind the gap

Sir, Only one London Underground station (letter, Nov 8) has six consonants consecutively in its name: Knightsbridge.

Robert Purdie Faringdon, Oxon

Sir, If I were quizmaster, I would not accept Alan Hadfield's answer. The station is South Ealing, not Ealing South.

Chris Bushill London N14

Tube teasers

Sir, Alan Hadfield's favourite quiz question (letters, Nov 8 & 9) is about London Underground stations and vowels. Mine is this: only one Underground station contains none of the letters in the word "mackerel". Pleasingly for cricket lovers, that station is St John's Wood.

Ian Jones Lingfield, Surrey

Sir, The longest London Underground station name in which all the letters are different is Wimbledon Park.

Michael Ross Exeter

Going underground

Sir, The letters about Tube stations (Nov 8–10) reminded me of one of my favourite quiz questions: "Which is the only Paris Metro station to share its exact name with a station on the London Underground?" The answer is Temple, both stations being named after their proximity to the original churches of the Knights Templar in Paris and in London.

Laurence Boynton Billingham, Co Durham

Sir, I wonder if those who spend their time seeking cryptic questions in the names of Tube stations usually get off at East Ham. Any Londoner can tell you this is only one stop short of Barking.

Bruce Hunt Linton, Cambs

Air mail

Sir, A padded envelope too large to go through the letterbox was left in front of a village front door ("Parcel thefts on the rise as 'porch pirates' target homes", news, Nov 18). I saw a cheeky gull grab the envelope in its mouth and fly off to the nearby churchyard. No criminal gangs here, merely opportunistic seagulls.

Susan McCormick Appledore, Devon

Motorway monotony

Sir, Your obituary of Penelope Hewitt (Nov 18) recalls how she eased the journey on the M62 by counting Eddie Stobart lorries. On the drive from Bath to Northampton my wife and I look for Home Bargains lorries. I doubt we are the only ones with this compulsion.

Michael Dawe Northampton

Sir, Michael Dawe (letter, Nov 22) and his wife relieve the tedium of motorway travel by looking out for Home Bargains lorries. He suggests that others may do the same. Each Morrisons lorry has a unique four-digit code on the back of the trailer. Some may be seen frequently while others are rare sightings. Just saying.

Robin Waldren Ashtead, Surrey

Motorway cricket

Sir, A cure for motorway monotony (letters, Nov 22 & 23) is HGV cricket. You can make up your own rules but one passenger bowls and another bats. Single runs are scored by every moving tanker passed, vehicles with orange flashing lights are two runs, car transporters are four and blue flashing lights are six. These can be augmented. The bowler can nominate three brands of lorries to be wickets, say Argos, Post Office and usually Eddie Stobart. We started playing this a few years ago as a substitute for pub cricket as there are not many pubs on motorways, or anywhere else now.

Edward Hine Newark, Notts

More motorway games

Sir, On the A34 it is easy to spot Home Bargains vehicles. Far more challenging is a game based on cricketers' names. Downton gets five points but a full name like Robert Croft (& Co) gets a full ten points.

Bernard White Ripon, N Yorks

Sir, A good way to ease the boredom of a car journey (letters, Nov 22–24) is to take the three letters of the numberplate of a car in front and make a word that uses the letters in that order. The longest word wins.

Wendy Ross Leeds

Sir, Further to ways of relieving tedium when driving (letters, Nov 22–25), here in the Chiltern area of outstanding natural beauty we count the HS2 lorries, in both directions, carrying excavation material. My record is 18 on a three-mile drive.

Richard Graham Great Missenden, Bucks

Power vacuum

Sir, Giles Coren's Laws of Domestic Management (Notebook, Dec 12) reminds me of my newly appointed cleaning lady asking for a second vacuum cleaner to be bought and kept upstairs to avoid her having to carry such a heavy load up and downstairs. I immediately agreed, but on further reflection thought her request to be excessive and perhaps a little presumptuous. When I told her so in slightly more tactful language, she nodded her approval with a smile and has carried out her duties excellently ever since.

Georgina Gatzen Chalfont St Giles, Bucks

Clean break

Sir, By refusing her cleaning lady's request for a second vacuum cleaner, Georgina Gatzen (letter, Dec 14; Giles Coren, Dec 12) has broken the Second Law of Domestic Management: cleaning ladies must have their way or they may leave to find more accommodating employers. I fear that by not only refusing a reasonable request but also by reneging on her initial agreement, Ms Gatzen has broken that law and may find that the cleaner's smile and nod was not what she thought but a note to herself to start looking for a new employer.

Sheena Mackay London SW14

Upstairs, downstairs

Sir, When I saw our cleaner heaving our vacuum cleaner upstairs (letters, Dec 14 & 15) I tried it myself and quickly decided to invest in a lightweight version, which stays upstairs. This proved a much safer solution and was much appreciated by our hard-working cleaner.

Tony Westhead Old Amersham, Bucks

Sir, During the pandemic, without cleaning help, my elderly parents found a neat solution to the problem of heaving the vacuum cleaner up and down stairs. They simply sent it up and down on their stairlift.

Dr Fiona Cornish Cambridge

Make it a double

Sir, Dr Fiona Cornish's parents carried their vacuum cleaner upstairs on their stairlift (letter, Dec 16). My father used his for himself and his nightly glass of whisky. His only complaint was that the stairlift went so slowly that he had finished the glass by the time it reached the landing and had to make the same journey again.

David Bickford London SW3

Delete to declutter

Sir, With predictable New Year gusto I have resolved to declutter my life and live more simply. For others wanting to do the same I strongly recommend aggressively reviewing the contact list on your PC or phone. This simple armchair exercise provides immense pleasure as you delete those people and organisations you happily need never engage with again. What a kick-start. It only need take an hour and it surely beats clearing out the garage or the loft.

Michael Brown Wallingford, Oxon

Sir, Great idea from Michael Brown to purge the contacts list for the new year (letter, Jan 1). I am going to apply four categories: 1, Friend; 2, Good acquaintance; 3, Would no longer cross road to say hello; and 4, *Who?*

Tim Soar Long Crendon, Bucks

Sexism street

Sir, With reference to the discomfort of some of the residents of Slag Lane ("Back to Slag Lane as divided village reinstates road signs", Jan 3), I was reminded of when we considered buying a house near Rye that I liked but my wife did not. The problem was the address: Dumb Woman's Lane. It didn't stop Spike Milligan from living there.

Nigel Webb Appledore, Kent

Retribution Lane

Sir, Further to the letter "Sexism Street" (Jan 5), rather than Dumb Woman's Lane denoting a stupid woman, the term was used to denote a well-known local gossip whose tongue was cut out by the Rye smugglers for informing on them.

Professor Sophie Watson Head of Sociology, Open University

Woolly thinking

Sir, Regarding Roland White's Thunderer, "Soon they will be telling us how to put on our jumpers" (Jan 16), my sister, who is in her mid-seventies, had a problem with her boiler. The young man who came to fix it noticed that the thermostat was not turned up very high. She responded that it was too expensive. "How do you manage when it's really cold then?" he said. She replied that she put on an extra jumper. He stared at her for a moment and then said: "Well, I suppose that *could* work."

Sally Bickersteth Alswear, Devon

Great scone debate

Sir, Susie Dent is correct that either way of pronouncing scone is fine ("Countdown host finally settles the great scone debate", Jan 18). There is an anonymous rhyme that sums it up: "I asked the maid in dulcet tone/ To order me a buttered scone./ The silly girl has been and gone/ And ordered me a buttered scone."

Ruth Wright Longborough, Glos

Fashion nightmare

Sir, Further to your article "It's not easy being tall (if you're a woman)" (Weekend, Jan 20), my mother and father were medium-tall, nothing to write home about. My husband is 6ft 6in, my son 6ft 2in and my two grandsons 6ft 3in and 6ft 4in respectively. At 5ft 8in I feel positively petite beside them, yet I still have trouble finding dresses, skirts and trousers long enough to fit.

Dr Vivien Graveson Darsham, Suffolk

Sir, I am 4ft 10in tall and take a size 2½ shoe. I can't remember the last time I was able to wear a dress, and even so-called "short-fitting" trousers have to be taken up a good four inches. I can assure your taller ladies that it's just as difficult down here as it is up there.

Pam Butcher Staines, Surrey

Lofty ideal

Sir, Oh, to be 5ft 8in (letter, Jan 25). With a husband of 6ft 5in, a daughter of 5ft 9in and a son of 6ft 2in, plus a brother and sister-in-law of 6ft 4in and 6ft 3in, I feel tiny in comparison at 5ft 3in. As for getting clothes to fit, everything is too long or has sleeves that completely cover my hands.

Nicky Gill Richmond, Surrey

Little and large

Sir, Some women bemoan being tall and others regret being small (letters, Jan 25–27). However, it could be worse: one can be both.

Roslyn Tall (5ft 2in) Potton, Beds

Fashion shortcuts

Sir, I am 5ft 3in but have no trouble finding clothes (letters, Jan 26, 27 & 29): I just buy off the teenage rail – no VAT and great modern choices. Today I am wearing the cast-off jeans of my 14-year-old great-grandson. I can't wait for him to have another clear-out.

Lesley Edmunds Netherton, Perth and Kinross

Retail satisfaction

Sir, I went to my local John Lewis department store in Milton Keynes this morning to buy a non-stick slotted spoon, a dishwasher cleaner and an affordable coffee grinder. I came away empty-handed. Having read your news report over lunch, "Latest John Lewis range hits the spot" (Feb 14), I realise that I should have been looking for Divine Glow Aqua Lubricant, Pure Delight Orgasm Balm and an Intimate Wand.

Thank you for the heads up.

David Thomas Great Denham, Beds

Spellbinding sales

Sir, Seeing Dr D G Hessayon's 96th birthday recorded in *The Times* (Feb 13) reminds me of when I encountered him in the 1990s at a Hatchards "authors of the year" party. I asked him how he could account for the fact that his many "Garden Expert" books were constantly in the bestselling charts and continued to sell tens of thousands of copies every year. "Cheap binding," he replied.

Joseph Connolly London NW3

Pointless artefacts

Sir, In his rant about washing-up bowls, Giles Coren ("Query the washing-up bowl and chaos awaits", Feb 17) asks what is the point of Swiss Army knives? I was given one for my 40th birthday. Soon afterwards we were on holiday on a Greek island, on a walk, when my daughter's flip-flop broke. The toe flange that goes down through a hole between the big toe and the "index" toe came loose. Using the hook on my Swiss Army knife, I was able to pull the flange back through the hole and the walk was saved. I have taken it on holiday with me ever since. The corkscrew came in useful as well.

Adrian Holroyd Kingswear, Devon

Sir, When my husband died, I took my sons to say goodbye to him at the undertaker's. One of them slipped his father's Swiss Army knife (letter, Feb 17) into his coffin. As he said, "he couldn't be without it".

Lady Hughes Wilburton, Cambs

Breaking the bank

Sir, When I asked my bank to change our joint account into my name only after my husband's death, I was asked for a copy of the death certificate. I had run out so proffered the grant of probate, pointing out it was difficult to obtain such without a death, but no, a death certificate it had to be. I ignored subsequent requests and eventually the bank capitulated, changing the account name from "Mr R Walsh Mrs S Walsh" to "Mrs S Walsh Mrs S Walsh".

Sally Walsh Bluntisham, Cambs

Sir, I endorse Emma Duncan's remarks about the efficiency of the systems for registering a death and the kindness of the people who operate them (Notebook, Mar 18). One young man slightly amended the "I'm sorry for your loss" mantra by saying "I apologise for your loss". It made me laugh (afterwards) – which is really the best therapy.

Pauline Droop London SW13

'Widow' trauma

Sir, I am sadly a widow but Lloyds need not be concerned that signs or advertisements for Scottish Widows will "trigger memories of trauma and upsetting situations" ("'Widow' is a no-no, says bank's guide", Mar 19). The bank seems to have an inflated view of its power. It's also a very odd use of words, as if bereavement is just one sole moment of death and not continuous. No signs or business names affect me but beautiful poetry, books, plays, art, the countryside and especially music most certainly do.

Sheila Meadows London SE19

Sir, I don't mind being called a widow. It's a statement of fact. Do I need counselling?

Sue Stevens Kingswear, Devon

Stairway to heaven

Sir, Further to your article on the benefit of taking the stairs ("A simple step to live longer – avoid taking the lift", Apr 27), as a fit 67-year-old I always choose the stairs and espouse the benefits to all who are prepared to listen. A sneaking part of me wonders, though, whether a careful analysis might reveal that the extra lifetime hours gained would turn out to have been spent climbing stairs.

Martyn Leadley Corfe Mullen, Dorset

Politics
and
history

Eton's failure

Sir, Whatever wider strategy Eton adopts, the school itself will continue to educate the global elite or those who will become the global elite ("If we'd stayed the same since 1440, Eton would have closed years ago", Jun 10). Perhaps its most important mission will be to ensure that its pupils are saved from the sense of privilege, entitlement and omniscience that can produce alumni such as Boris Johnson, Jacob Rees-Mogg, Kwasi Kwarteng and Ben Elliot and thereby damage a country's very fabric. Sadly, I failed in that purpose.

John Claughton Master, Eton College, 1984–2001

Hamming it up

Sir, I don't know if it's my age, but my first thought when I saw the headline "To move on, consign this vain man to spam" (comment, Jun 12) was that Max Hastings was suggesting that Boris Johnson should be made into the cheap tinned food containing pork, ham and salt.

Keith Brown Lanchester, Co Durham

Gardening leave

Sir, Professor Ian Kunkler (letter, Jun 13) suggests that Boris Johnson may be hoping to emulate the Roman general Camillus in staging a comeback. May I suggest that he instead model himself on the Emperor Diocletian, who, when urged by his followers to return to power, refused, saying that he would much prefer to remain in retirement growing cabbages. I, for one, would willingly contribute towards the cost of an allotment.

Guy Morpuss KC Farnham, Surrey

Bozymandias

Sir, I met a traveller from an EU land/ Who said: "Two vast and trunkless legs of stone/ Stand in Westminster. Near them, on the Strand, / Half sunk, a shatter'd visage lies, whose hair/ And fat lip, and leer of false command, / Tell that its sculptor well those passions read/ Which yet survive, stamped on these lifeless things,/ The hand that mock'd them, and the heart that fed; /And on the pedestal, these words appear: 'My name is Bozymandias, PM of PMs; / Look on my works, ye Mighty, and despair!' / Nothing beside remains. Round the decay/ Of that colossal wreck, boundless and bare, / Bruised Britain stretches far away."

Kevin Deeming Farnham, Surrey. Adapted from the poem by Percy Bysshe Shelley

Lonely exile

Sir, After his final defeat in 1815 Napoleon Bonaparte was forced into exile on the island of St Helena in the South Atlantic, where he was guarded by members of the 53rd (Shropshire) Regiment of Foot. He remained there until his death in 1821. Maybe Boris Johnson could be forced into a similar exile, but one less comfortable. Rockall, perhaps? The North Atlantic outcrop has the benefit that no soldiers would be needed to guard him – or listen to his bombast.

Anna Brown Sheffield

Model application

Sir, My wife, Kari-Ann, who is Norwegian, has lived in the UK for 74 years but is now being asked to apply to the EU settlement scheme, so to support her application I have uploaded a picture of Roxy Music's 1972 debut album, *Roxy Music*, as she is featured on the cover. I wonder if this is admissible evidence?

Chris Jagger Mudgley, Somerset

Blood bank

Sir, In Bram Stoker's novel the protagonist, Jonathan Harker, examines Dracula's correspondence and says that "the third [letter] was to Coutts & Co, London". This raises the interesting question of whether Coutts has become more rigorous since the end of the 19th century, or whether its opinion of Nigel Farage is even lower than we have been led to believe ("Farage says bank accounts were closed 'to force me out of UK'", Jun 30).

Julian Critchlow Ditcham, Hants

Junior accounting

Sir, I was surprised in July 1984 to receive, from Barclays Bank, a request for a character reference for my week-old daughter, in whose name I had attempted to open a deposit account. I replied: "She is illiterate, inarticulate and incontinent. These shortcomings aside, I can thoroughly recommend her to you." The bank agreed to open the account. The next day I closed it.

Professor David Clark Ashow, Warks

Infant layabout

Sir, Further to the letter from Professor David Clark, after the birth of our grandson in hospital in New Zealand his parents were given a document that, among other things, described him as "aged 1 day", "single" and "unemployed".

Edward Cole Craven Arms, Shropshire

Braverman's future

Sir, In your story about Suella Braverman ("No 10's Suella dilemma: keep in or cast out?", Aug 19) you describe her as a polarising figure, with some of her colleagues deriding her as "totally useless" and others hailing her as a future party leader. I'd like to point out that, based on recent experience, the one doesn't rule out the other.

Ian Jones Lingfield, Surrey

Rail kiosk closures

Sir, Some years ago I took my mother to Harrogate bus station. A lady in front of us asked question after question and delayed us. When we got to the ticket office the cashier said: "She comes in every week and asks the same questions." I remarked: "That's a bit strange", but my mother, ever more intuitive than me, replied: "That's probably the only conversation she has all week." There are hidden benefits of personal service.

Andy Brewer London W4

Long memories

Sir, Your leading article on Australia's "Voice" referendum ("Royal Pardon", Oct 16) speaks of a monarchy's value and advises, if it ain't broke, mate, don't fix it. Stronger advice was given to a visiting American teacher at my school in the early Sixties. He had suggested to an assembly of teachers that it was time that Britain got up to date and appointed a president. After a moment's pause, one teacher pointed out that we had tried this 300 years ago and that it had taken us only 12 years to realise that we had made a mistake.

Peter Inson East Mersea, Essex

Odd denomination

Sir, I agree with Julian Barnes that it may be time to take copper coins out of circulation (letter, Oct 16), but in light of prevalent retail practice ought the Royal Mint to issue a 99p coin?

Malcolm Rogers Broadway, Worcs

Short-changed

Sir, Malcolm Rogers's suggestion of a 99p coin (letter, Oct 18) would defeat the original purpose of pricing this way. Items at 19 shillings and 11 pence were once common. This aimed to force the shop assistant to open the till and give a penny change, thereby registering the sale. A £1 item could result in the note being slipped into a pocket – "to put in the till when we're less busy" – and then "forgotten" about.

Richard Shaw Prestatyn, north Wales

Pocketing pennies

Sir, Further to the correspondence about a 99p coin (letters, Oct 18 & 19), as a student working in a bar in the early 1970s I was once taken aside by the landlord after I had served a round of drinks that came to exactly £1. "Always add a penny or two to the total," he said. When I asked why, he said that "£1.02 sounds much more accurate and precise than a pound – and less likely to be challenged."

Professor David Stephens Brighton

Drinking culture

Sir, It is not just abusive behaviour that is a problem ("Culture of drinking in Westminster 'fuelling abusive behaviour by MPs'", Oct 18, and letter, Oct 19). Westminster is a workplace where our elected representatives make decisions that affect all of us. Why anyone thinks that it is a good idea to facilitate those decisions being made while under the influence of alcohol is beyond me. Shutting the bars on the parliamentary estate is long overdue.

Sir Peter Rubin Lay member of the Commons committee on standards, 2016–20

Ruled by drink

Sir, Sir Peter Rubin thinks it unwise for MPs to make decisions while under the influence of alcohol (letter, Oct 20). According to Herodotus, the ancient Persians would disagree. They would deliberate on important matters while drunk, and then reconsider on the following day when sober; only if the same result was achieved on both occasions would the decision stand. Of course, this does require that there are at least some days of abstinence.

Geoff Wilkins Brixworth, Northants

Silence is golden

Sir, James Marriott's excellent piece on today's glut of self-important and ill-informed comment ("You don't need to share your views on Gaza", Nov 2) reminds me of an aphorism by the great American TV news anchor Walter Cronkite: "I never learnt anything while I was talking."

Gavin Shreeve London W4

Streets ahead

Sir, Sathnam Sanghera's concerns about a lack of imagination in street-naming are misplaced (Notebook, Nov 13) – at least in the Brighton Hill area of Basingstoke where I learnt to drive almost 30 years ago. I well remember the challenges of an uphill start on Brahms Road, stalling perennially on Stravinsky Road and reversing around the corner into Mahler Close. The driving test centre remains, as it was in the 1990s, across the road from Handel Close. And lest any burgher of Basingstoke should fear the town planners were being too diverse or international in their choices, the discerning learner driver can always practise their parking on Lennon Way or McCartney Walk.

George Cazenove London, SW6

Sir, One of the best examples of imaginative street naming (letter, Nov 14) is the address for the South Yorkshire Police Operations Complex: Letsby Avenue, Sheffield.

Robert Evans Weybridge, Surrey

Sir, For your disinformation, the Russian embassy in Dublin is on Orwell Road.

Cherrie Coghlan Cottenham, Cambs

Sir, Like George Cazenove (letter, Nov 14), I too admire the Basingstoke planners' imagination in naming streets after musicians and composers. Sadly, while there is a Dankworth Road they never took the opportunity to create a Cleo Lane.

Chris Duckling Bexhill-on-Sea, E Sussex

Roman sex change

Sir, The reputation of the emperor Elagabalus was shredded by the contemporary historian Dio and by later writers ("Roman emperor was trans woman, declares museum", Nov 22). We can no longer decipher behind the polemic whether he would have claimed to be trans. But we do know that the Romans recognised that sex change was possible. Pliny in his encyclopaedic *Natural History* reports cases of women turning into men, including one actually at a wedding he had attended. Their views of gender weren't ours, but they were surprisingly fluid.

Andrew Wallace-Hadrill Honorary professor of Roman studies, Cambridge University

DNA test for bones of Princes in the Tower

Sir, Alice Loxton concludes her article on the Princes in the Tower with a reference to the bones in Westminster Abbey, which are thought by some to be those of the princes ("Medieval murder mystery still divides us", comment, Nov 25). These bones were uncovered by workmen in the Tower of London in 1674, during the reign of Charles II. The King believed they deserved a more reverent burial, and they were thus transferred to the abbey. But were they – are they – the real thing? In this age of DNA it should be possible to find out. I would therefore urge our present King, with his great knowledge of and interest in history, to arrange for this test. King Charles III could solve at last the mystery of King Richard III, which has teased historians for so long.

Lady Antonia Fraser London W8

Darling's wit

Sir, Alistair Darling (obituary, Dec 1) possessed a wonderfully self-effacing sense of humour. Shortly after he was appointed chancellor, he told me that he had been horrified to hear on the *Today* programme that the chancellor would be making a major speech later that day. He spent the next few moments trying to figure out "what on earth Gordon was going to be talking about" before remembering that he was now the chancellor and would be the person giving the speech.

Dr Norman Fraser Cambridge

Move over, Darling

Sir, Shortly after Labour lost the 2010 general election I happened to be on the Heathrow to Edinburgh shuttle with both Alistair Darling (obituary, Dec 1; letter, Dec 2) and Gordon Brown, who were sitting apart. Mr Brown, as a former prime minister, was accompanied by personal security, and when a delay in the flight meant we all had to return to the terminal he was whisked away to a VIP area. Mr Darling, meanwhile, stood with the crowd at the departure gate, happily and affably chatting to everyone. Politicians are human beings, but some are more human than others.

Gareth Howlett Edinburgh

Legacy of marriage

Sir, Is an enduring monogamous marriage an impediment to achieving success and celebrity? Of the 897 obituaries *The Times* published in 2023, the majority were for persons married more than once, divorced or separated or never married at all. Only 47 per cent were for persons married only once, and that drops below 40 per cent when excluding those who lived a large part of their adult lives independently, having either been widowed early or married late. It does not bode well for my wife and me – happily together after 53 years – to ever feature.

Jeffrey Golden KC London SW13

Sir, I think that Jeffrey Golden KC has things the wrong way round (letters, Jan 1). It is not that "enduring monogamous marriage" is "an impediment to achieving success and celebrity", but rather that success and celebrity are an impediment to enduring monogamous marriage. Your pages seem to bear this out almost daily with their tales of the marital histories of successful and celebrated people.

Timothy Reynolds Cranleigh, Surrey

Bearskin necessity

Sir, As an environmentalist, Stephen Fry may be pleased to know that His Majesty's Guards have a long tradition of recycling their bearskin caps ("Fry condemns bearskin 'shame'", Jan 11). When I joined the Welsh Guards I inherited my grandfather's bearskin, which he first wore in 1923. When I left the army my bearskin was handed down and is still worn today. About 95 per cent of bearskins worn today have belonged to previous Guardsmen. Bearskin caps last and hold their shape beautifully.

Paul de Zulueta London W8

Sir, What Paul de Zulueta will know (letter, Jan 12), and Stephen Fry almost certainly won't (report, Jan 11), is that bearskins are multi-purpose. When on King's Guard at St James's Palace, two officers out of the three on duty are allowed to swim in the Royal Automobile Club's indoor pool in Pall Mall. To go there they must be properly dressed in bearskin, tunic and sword. But not, obviously, allowed to carry a parcel. So, rather than having a Guardsman take their bathing trunks there (towels are provided), they secrete their Speedos inside their bearskin caps. This is fine but the return journey with wet trunks can present problems.

Michael Scott Formerly of the Scots Guards; London W1

Sir, Michael Scott (letter, Jan 13) is right to point out bearskins' multi-purpose role. When I did my first guard at the Tower of London, I dutifully carried out my tour of the sentries in the early hours. It was eerily quiet, the mist swirling up from the Thames through Traitors' Gate; visions of beheaded corpses popping up from behind a turret were close to mind. A brother officer, however, anxious to test my steadiness on parade, had hidden a small alarm clock in my bearskin. As I rounded Traitors' Gate, the alarm went off. It was good training for a tour six months later in South Armagh at the height of the Troubles.

William McLean Formerly of the Coldstream Guards, Eyton on Severn, Shropshire

Fit for a king

Sir, I was dismayed to read that the King's official portrait is to hang outside head teachers' offices (report, Jan 16). A former colleague used to tell pupils imperiously: "The bursar has an office; teachers have studies."

John Hayes Cardiff

Moderating effect

Sir, Further to the article "Keir shouldn't make decisions with only men in the room" (*Times2*, Jan 29), I once asked a Maori woman why women were not allowed to speak in the meeting house. She replied that it was not necessary but that they must be present. I asked if the women lobbied the men beforehand. She responded that this was not necessary either. I waited, puzzled. She then said: "Our presence is essential. It modifies the men's behaviour but also their thinking. For us, that is enough."

Hilary Elfick Cambridge

Criticism of Diana

Sir, In an excerpt from *Tatler* reprinted in *The Times*, Lady Venetia Baring alleges that my late mother, the Dowager Countess of Cromer, said "she really didn't like Diana" and that "Diana should get a grip" ("Queen's aide 'thought Diana should get a grip'", Jan 25). My mother served the late Queen for 17 years and was rewarded for her loyalty, work and affection by a CVO. Throughout her long service my mother was the soul of discretion, no doubt learnt from her years as wife of a governor of the Bank of England and wife of a British ambassador to Washington. It would be totally alien to my mother to make a comment on a member of the royal family to anybody, least of all to one of her grandchildren and especially to Lady Venetia Baring, my daughter, who was born after the death of Diana, Princess of Wales.

The Earl of Cromer Bangkok

Clinic or theatre?

Sir, Dr JRD Laycock (letter, Feb 8) asks how it can be right that a specialist in adult cognitive behaviour is paid the same as a consultant cardiac surgeon. I agree. A cognitive behaviour therapist's work is far more draining than surgery and should be rewarded accordingly. Clinic or theatre? Most of us surgeons would prefer the operating room any day.

Daryl Godden Consultant maxillofacial head and neck reconstructive surgeon, Painswick, Glos

Pavement politics

Sir, Laura Freeman's excellent and heartfelt column "Let's stop this civic death by a thousand cuts" (Feb 14) strikes a huge chord in Camden. For almost 30 years, I have lived in a street that is half York paving and half concrete slabs, after the council ripped up the old paving stones without consultation. The York paving has lasted better, and is markedly less strewn with rubbish than the latter. It also has better trees. I can't but wonder whether citizens unconsciously take more care of beautiful pavements than ugly ones.

Amanda Craig London NW1

Royal blood line

Sir, Sadiq Khan should have continued the tradition of naming London railway lines after the royal family, as in Victoria and Elizabeth ("Is £6m rail rebrand an own goal?" news, Feb 16). There are plenty of likely suspects for inspiration: The Andrew Line, The Harry Line, The Meghan Line, to name but three.

Viv Mercer Southport, Merseyside

Going underground

Sir, Rather than naming London Overground stations after here today, gone tomorrow political and sporting subjects (letter, Feb 17; news, Feb 16), surely it would be better to name them after London's long-established but now largely hidden rivers, such as the Walbrook, Stamford, Effra, Fleet, Tyburn and Ravensbourne.

Andrew Luff London NW1

Fear of Old Boney

Sir, When talking about Putin's legacy, Matthew Parris ("Dreams and darkness: how Ukraine's young people really feel", Feb 17) refers to his grandmother closing his bedroom windows 150 years after the battle of Trafalgar "or Old Boney will get you". My 88-year-old mother recently came to stay and when I suggested we leave the bedroom curtains open a chink to let the fresh air in, she was appalled. She recounted how every night of her life she had shut the curtains wherever she was "or Herr Hitler would see the light and know where to drop his bombs". As Parris says of Putin: "There can be no moving on from this."

Lorna Robson Clench, Wilts

North by northeast

Sir, I wondered why James Marriott singled out Sunderland in his piece "Why the south now just ignores the north" (Feb 22). Reading on revealed that he grew up in Newcastle; presumably, then, a Newcastle United supporter. Rivalry between Newcastle and Sunderland began with the coal trade, carried on in the Civil War and continues today in football. Sunderland deserves a better understanding of its history: its shipyards produced more than a quarter of Britain's merchant ships in the Second World War. On a cultural level, it is the birthplace of the Venerable Bede and the source of the Codex Amiatinus.

Peter McKenzie Morpeth, Northumberland

Sir, James Marriott makes a compelling case that southerners ignore the north. Just wait until somebody tells them about the existence of the Midlands.

Alexander Titcomb Nottingham

Sir, With reference to the north-south divide (Feb 22; letters, Feb 23), the great expanse of land in the US between east and west coasts is often derisively referred to as "the flyover". The Midlands is surely England's equivalent – "the drive-through"?

Mart Ralph Salisbury

Sir, I was at AFC Wimbledon recently and an AFC player was felled by an agricultural tackle from an opponent. A section of the crowd chanted "You dirty northern bastards". The opposition was Mansfield.

Neil Withington London SW20

Sir, Further to Neil Withington's letter about Wimbledon AFC fans (Feb 26), I grew up watching Plymouth Argyle in the 1970s. We chanted "You dirty northern bastards" at *every* visiting team, safe in the knowledge that geography was on our side.

Gerard Bell Ascot

Table manners

Sir, Jonathan Morrison says that the revolving restaurant at the top of the Post Office Tower "never really reopened" after it was bombed by the IRA in 1971 ("Towering symbol to become a hotel", Feb 22). I have a written record of my visit to the restaurant in December 1977. The restaurant was on the 57th floor, the lavatories on the 58th. On returning from the facilities, one had to search for one's table as it was no longer where one had left it.

Alec Gallagher Potton, Beds

Church and slavery

Sir, Further to the Church of England's reparations for past slavery ("Church told to build £1bn slavery reparations fund", Mar 5), for the first three years of my 40 years of ministry in the C of E I was paid nothing. Slavery? For almost ten years after I retired I took services to make up for lack of stipendiary clergy. I was supposed to be paid a fee for this, plus expenses. Was I? Not a penny. My clergy pension has been cut from what I was promised. Yet the rich Church Commissioners, who plead poverty about restoring my pension entitlement while expecting me to work for them for nothing, can give millions of pounds away. Slavery? Who are they trying to fool?

Father Allan Campbell-Wilson Scarborough, N Yorks

Sir, Laura Lockwood is fortunate indeed to have been offered a £2 increase on her £45 service fee as an organist. Once a year after the Christmas Eve carol service I am affectionately presented with six bottles of wine and six bottles of beer, which are promptly drunk by my visiting sons. There has been no increase in 18 years but I do note that the cost of wine and beer has risen.

Melanie Carroll Organist, Oare Church, Somerset

Making work pay

Sir, It is sometimes said that the problem with British politics is that we want European levels of public services with American levels of taxation. It is the singular dismal achievement of our present government that we somehow have American levels of public services with European levels of taxation.

Andrew Roy KC 12 King's Bench Walk, London EC4

Enemy at the gates

Sir, Kathleen Tebb (letter, Mar 6) argues that Chris Packham and his ilk are wrong to believe that they have any right to protest outside politicians' homes, on the grounds that the principle is that "an Englishman's home is his castle". But the function of a castle was to prevent hostile people forcing an entrance into one's home – nobody ever bothered to build a castle unless they expected hostile people to turn up from time to time and attempt this. It could never prevent an enemy from simply besieging it; the occupants simply had to sit tight and hope the besiegers would eventually give up and go away. Sieges of castles were far commoner in medieval warfare than battles, so in fact the protesters, rather than Ms Tebb, are the ones upholding the letter and the spirit of this particular principle.

Victoria Solt Dennis Brompton, Kent

Keeping Britain tidy

Sir, Jenni Russell ("Our litter-choked roads are a national disgrace", Mar 18) highlights that both the causes and the effects of widespread roadside litter need to be addressed. On the M3 south of the M25 it is more than a year since the central reservation kerbs were cleared of debris, allowing last year's seeds and saplings to take root in the detritus. Among the dead animals and shredded tyres there is no doubt plenty of red tape, in which the agencies and authorities responsible are gratefully concealing themselves.

Richard Blamey Teffont Evias, Wilts

Sir, Whoever runs for election under Jenni Russell's slogan "Make Britain clean again" will get my vote. The mayor of Trieste was elected under a similar banner in Italy and tourism has flourished, along with roadside flowers.

Tom Perry Marlow, Bucks

Sir, Recently I was being driven along the highway just outside Johannesburg and witnessed several controlled small fires by the side of the road. The driver told me that this was the authorities' way of dealing with roadside litter. It appeared to be very effective.

Jonathan Carey Weston, Hants

Sir, I had just arrived in Japan and was unaware of the unwritten rule that I should carry my own bag for collecting my daily rubbish to take home. I bought a cup of tea at a station and fished out the teabag. Holding the boiling hot teabag I ran round the station looking for a litter bin. No litter bin. I still feel guilty for stuffing it behind a pipe; it was that or burning my fingers. I just hope it was a biodegradable teabag.

Shelagh Fitzpatrick Teddington

Sir, Highways England might look at following the example of the road sign erected by New Zealand's transport department across the country: "Don't be a tosser. Bin it!"
It seems to work.

Mike Wicksteed Caterham, Surrey

Don't be a tosser

Sir, Further to Mike Wicksteed's letter on deterring roadside litter in New Zealand (Mar 20), the village of Ashley in Cheshire has had signs saying "Don't be a tosser" for a number of years. It helps but sadly does not solve the problem.

Peter Hardern Bowden, Greater Manchester

Men only

Sir, I have often been a guest at the Garrick Club and have always been made welcome. I have no desire to be a member – why pay for pleasures that are free? I would like to think that male guests at women-only clubs are accorded the same gracious hospitality. But I would not like men to be members of our clubs lest they spoil the atmosphere with their cigars. This is a tempest in a teapot and has nothing of real significance to say about women's rights ("Civil service and MI6 chiefs resign from all-male Garrick Club", Mar 21). Those who are making a fuss about it might better turn their attention to preventing sexual crimes against women or discrimination in the workforce rather than rail against a group of probably the most interesting and accomplished men in London.

Elise Becket-Smith Oxford

Sir, Regarding your discussion of the Garrick Club's membership ("Garrick is sent list of seven women who should be admitted", Mar 29), a colleague who is gay, a former barrister and an established playwright recounted the time when he endured a member moaning that the club was "full of lawyers, theatre people and homosexuals". He raised his hand and said: "House!"

Colin Mayes London NW6

Sir, My father, Richard Hough, was a lifelong Garrick member, and in fact wrote a history of the club. One evening he overheard a chap at the bar saying: "I've only been into my wife's kitchen twice, and once was to put out a fire." Says it all really.

Deborah Moggach London NW5

Risk-taking MPs

Sir, Ann Jenkin makes a good point in differentiating between the male and female appetite for taking unnecessary risks ("It's only male MPs who take these career-ending risks", Thunderer, Apr 22). Having managed a business that recruited highly qualified graduates to trade in financial products, I was always surprised by how many applicants said they loved pressure and taking risks. I used to ask them whether they would like their doctors or train drivers to have the same enthusiasm for taking risk. No female applicants made the same pitch.

Hugh Cooper London SW4

Country
ways

Inspiring rambles

Sir, When praising tinkering in garages, garden sheds and attics (leading article, Jun 1), we should spare a thought for rambling: in 1941 George de Mestral found burdock burrs clinging to his clothing (and dog) in the Alps, and in 1967 Godfrey Hounsfield thought up computed tomography on a country walk. Imagine life without Velcro and CT medical imaging.

Tim Williams Waldron, E Sussex

Stingingly cold

Sir, In your leading article on snorkelling in Scottish waters, you rightly identify the underwater landscape as pristine ("Bonnie Snorkelling", Jun 5). Having just spent two weeks sailing through the Inner and Outer Hebrides I can confirm that the sea at this time of year is remarkable not only for its clarity but also for its abundance of jellyfish: lion's mane, purple stingers, barrel, compass and moon were in bloom. Although none of these splendid creatures can impart anything more than an unpleasant sting, they did provide a very good excuse for avoiding the risk of hypothermia from a bracing swim with or without a snorkel.

Dr Tim Fooks West Chiltington, W Sussex

Brew up for slugs

Sir, I'm surprised you did not mention in your article about the Royal Horticultural Society recommending that we embrace slugs (news, Jun 29), the perfect, eco-friendly antidote: garlic brew. Boil two bulbs of garlic in two litres of water, mash when soft and strain. Two tablespoons per watering can and hey presto – no slugs. I know they are part of nature's rich tapestry so I allow them to munch to their hearts' content in my wild area. It has saved my sweet peas, dahlias and lilies.

Susan Seely Worsley, Greater Manchester

Inventive rooks

Sir, The German rooks whose new harvesting habits in Bavaria you report on ("Rooks hatch new plan to pilfer crops", Aug 2) must have friends or relations here in Somerset. I have been watching a couple of hundred rooks using precisely the same methodology to feed themselves and their young for the past six or eight weeks in Lytes Cary: they walk into the field and push over the stalks, then eat the grains on the ground. I am sure the unsuspecting farmer will have a rude awakening when he gets down to the bottom of his field and finds it flattened, with no ears on the wheat.

Jeremy Hall Northover, Somerset

Resourceful rooks

Sir, Rooks in Bavaria must be really thick if they have only just worked out how to pilfer crops (world, Aug 2; letter, Aug 3). I have been working in UK farming since 1965: English rooks have always known how to walk into crops and push them over to get at the grain in the seed head.

Malcolm McAllister Lavenham, Suffolk

Nessie dormant

Sir, It is unlikely that the unexplained "distinctive noises" heard underwater in Loch Ness (report, Aug 28) are caused by a large animal unknown to science but that is no reason to stop looking. As Sir Peter Scott said, the only way to exclude the existence of the Loch Ness Monster is to drain all the water out of the loch and see what is left on the bottom.

Gareth Williams Author, *A Monstrous Commotion: the Mysteries of Loch Ness*

Elusive Nessie

Sir, Alas, draining Loch Ness (letter, Aug 29) would not resolve the debate over Nessie's existence as the northern end connects to Loch Dochfour via the River Ness, which ultimately leads to the North Sea via the Moray Firth. If Nessie is not found in residence she will simply have gone to visit her cousin Morag in Loch Morar.

Michael Pacione Milton of Campsie, E Dunbartonshire

Monster trip

Sir, Should Nessie exist she is likely to be a type of plesiosaur so it's very unlikely that she could navigate from the sea to Loch Ness by the river as it is too shallow (letter, Aug 30). However, should she exist she could return from her holidays via the canal – assuming that people are willing to help her through the locks.

Colin Macduff-Duncan Oxshott, Surrey

Asian hornet threat

Sir, The Asian hornet is a new and very serious threat to everyone, not just beekeepers ("Invasive species cost £336 billion a year – and problem is growing", Sep 5). It preys on honey bees and other pollinating insects, and in France there has been a decrease of 40 per cent in honey sales due to its presence. More importantly, we already have a massive decline in pollinators and anything that adds to that decline will cause huge problems for farmers and ultimately to all of us. One third of our food is dependent on pollinators. As I write, members of our association are volunteering a week of their time visiting Jersey, learning how to bait and track Asian hornets. There is no doubt that the Asian hornet is here: it is spreading so fast that we may be overcome.

Pauline Lane Secretary, Guildford Beekeepers Association

Bedbug renaissance

Sir, We worry a lot about the decline in biodiversity so we should welcome the news from France about bedbugs making a public comeback after their alleged extinction there ("Bedbug nuisance gets under people's skin", Sep 6), appearing not only in cinemas but on the Marseilles Metro. The French are in good company. More than a decade ago bedbugs turned up in New York in the Empire State Building, at the Metropolitan Opera House and on subway stations in Brooklyn, Manhattan and the Bronx.

The French blame international travel for their reintroduction. This is not a new hypothesis. As John Southall said in his 1730 *A Treatise of Buggs*: "By shipping they were doubtless first brought to England, so are they now daily brought." Perhaps they have travelled to France from Dundee, whose ladies in 1947 suffered from an epidemic of red bands of blisters on the back of their calves: they had been bitten by bugs living in a groove on the seats of a tram. Men escaped; Harris tweed trousers were too thick for the bedbugs' beaks.

Hugh Pennington Aberdeen

Ballooning anger

Sir, We livestock farmers have several names for a collection of hot air balloons (Notebook, Sep 9). We use them a lot while collecting and calming stampeding animals, and they are all unrepeatable in a respectable newspaper.

Charlie Flindt Hinton Ampner, Hants

Gone with the wind

Sir, I'm with Ann Treneman (Notebook, Sep 9): I was initially troubled by wind turbines but now the sight of them has an effect similar to that of church spires – a feeling of wellbeing. Even, perhaps, of hope.

Lucy Johnson Langport, Somerset

Wind of change

Sir, Obviously Ann Treneman (Sep 9) and Lucy Johnson (letter, Sep 12) don't live too near wind turbines. We are 3 miles from ours and when the wind is blowing towards us, which is quite often, it is dreadful. The whirring just goes on and on and on. And now more, even bigger, are proposed on the other side of the house.

Carol Gilmour Altass, Sutherland

Hiccups remedies

Sir, Among the various cures you suggest for hiccups (*Times2*, Oct 3) there was no mention of one sure-fire way of stopping them. This is to drink a full glass of water without stopping while blocking both ears. It is possible to do this by oneself, but of course it is much easier if someone else slowly tilts the glass. This method was taught by my biology master in the 1950s, Humphrey Moore, who was an expert on toads. He contended that if it didn't work you must be an amphibian.

Andrew Stronach Sevenoaks, Kent

Sir, When I was a teacher an attack of hiccups did occasionally occur in my class (*Times2*, Oct 3). A certain cure was to draw the attention of the whole class to the hiccuper by inviting them to listen to the hiccup "performance". It never failed.

Margaret Filsell Amersham, Bucks

Sir, Drinking from the wrong side of a glass of water works every time – and you don't need someone else to hold the glass (letter, Oct 4).

Christine McCann Bath

Sir, My schoolmaster taught me how to cure hiccups: take out a £20 note and hand it to the hiccupper the next time they hiccup. I have done this many times and they never do.

David Emmet London W5

Sir, Andrew Stronach's suggested cure for hiccups (letter, Oct 4), of drinking a glass of water while blocking both ears, sounds more like an opportunity for a cold soaking to me. My failsafe cure for hiccups is to try to remember what you had for dinner a week ago.

Penny Braithwaite Winslow, Bucks

Sir, The cure for hiccups which works every time for me is to swallow a tablespoon of vinegar.

David Roberts Gillingham, Dorset

Sir, When I was in my twenties, if I had hiccups (letters, Oct 4–7 & 9) I would ask one of my (male) flatmates to grab my feet and turn me upside down. This was 100 per cent successful.

Suzie Marwood London SW6

Sir, When I was a junior doctor, my consultant gave me invaluable advice: treat your patient's hiccups however you like, but do it quickly. If you don't, the patient will recover by herself/himself, and you'll get no credit.

Jeremy Roussak Manchester

Sir, A sweeter cure for hiccups (letters, Oct 4–7) is to crunch a sugar cube, or if that is unavailable, a teaspoonful of granulated sugar. If this is not immediately successful, repeat the exercise. It never fails.

Sue Matthews Epsom, Surrey

Sir, A sure-fire way to stop hiccups (letter, Oct 4–7, 9 & 10) is to think of a green horse in a white field: the concentration required renders the hiccups impotent.

Maggie Chilton Chipping Norton, Oxon

Cracking idea

Sir, Robert Crampton hankers after being able to crack a walnut in his hand (*Beta Male* magazine, Oct 7). He will find greater admiration if he throws a walnut at a plate-glass window, for it will break up on impact and leave the glass intact, however hard the walnut is thrown.

Malcolm Watson Ryde, Isle of Wight

Sir, With the imminent arrival of the Queen and Duke of Edinburgh for dinner on board HMS Blake in 1968, the ship's captain, Roland Plugge, a keen cricketer, visited the wardroom to check on the arrangements (which were of course perfect). On his way out he saw a bowl of walnuts (*Beta Male*, Oct 7; letter, Oct 9) and said: "Not many of you will know this, but you can chuck one as hard as you like at glass and it will not break it." With his bowling arm he then hurled a walnut at the large picture of the Queen behind her dining chair. The glass shattered. "Well, it normally works" was his only comment as he left, leaving the wardroom mess secretary two minutes to sort out the mess.

Vice-Admiral Sir Michael Moore Portchester, Hants

Sir, A second walnut held in the hand solves the problem; one or other (or both) will crack.

Christopher Gardner-Thorpe Consultant neurologist, Exeter

Sir, Simply insert a kitchen knifepoint into the "bottom" of a walnut and twist. No cracking required (letters, Oct 9 & 10). I gather thousands from my trees.

Phillip Hodson Tetbury, Glos

Fiddler on the roof

Sir, Further to the correspondence (Oct 9–11) about cracking walnuts, last year we found a number of neat round holes in our polycarbonate conservatory roof. The culprit? Local jackdaws sitting on the chimney, which dropped walnuts to crack them for their lunch. Maybe we should re-roof with plate glass.

Ruth Fearnley Drayton, Oxon

Squirrelled away

Sir, Sathnam Sanghera's squirrel problem (Notebook, Oct 16) is, sadly, commonplace. Two elderly residents of my village used to vie with each other every year for the most grey squirrels taken. One used an air rifle and the other a humane trap from which the live animal was extracted and then dispatched via her rainwater butt. They never reached the desired century but most years took more than 80 each. We have a very efficient machine mounted on an apple tree; carcasses are put into our council "green waste" bin.

Janet Hutson North Ferriby, E Yorks

Sir, I have a bird feeder, which so far the squirrels have not penetrated, so I am not driven squirrel nutkins on that score. But the parakeets of west London can empty it in a day.

Timothy George London W4

Biblical rain

Sir, These named storms surely provide scope for something less wimpy than Debi, Agnes or Minnie. Why not plunder the Old Testament and name them Methuselah, Meshach, Shadrach or Abednego among others? Perhaps the next one could be Ezekiel. Those names sound like proper storms and would lend them gravitas.

Clare Hallam Crosby Garrett, Cumbria

Sir, I have noticed that since our meteorologists started naming them, storms have become more frequent and more violent. To give them names "plundered from the Old Testament" (letter, Nov 15) would inevitably puff them up even more, creating weather of biblical extremes.

John Gifford Hutton Rudby, N Yorks

Sir, Rather than naming storms after biblical characters (letter, Nov 15 & 17) why not call them Boris, Liz, Rishi, Suella, etc? And, if a huge storm comes across the Atlantic, Donald.

David Price Cockermouth, Cumbria

Sir, Shadrach, Meshach and Abednego should not become storm names (letter, Nov 15). Their names should be reserved for heatwaves: they were in the fiery furnace with Daniel, so should know something about the effects of heat.

Roy Jones West Horsley, Surrey

Trial by fire

Sir, Roy Jones (letter, Nov 20) should consult Daniel iii: it was only Shadrach, Meshach and Abednego who were put into the fiery furnace, and not Daniel.

Kate Aitchison Edinburgh

Linear forest

Sir, The government has asked the public to nominate places for the creation of a new forest ("Forest for the nation looks for location", Nov 27). I propose the entire length of the cancelled northern legs of HS2. At least that way we will have something to show for the hundreds of millions of pounds spent on the purchase of land and houses along the route. It could be named the Phoenix Forest and contain a long-distance footpath called the "Permanent Way" as a reminder of the originally intended use and the fiasco it became.

Gordon Lethbridge Sherborne, Dorset

Eradicating stoats on Orkney

Sir, It took 24 professional trappers only nine years to eradicate 34,000 non-native coypu from East Anglia in the 1980s ("Halt £16m scheme to kill Orkney stoats, urge insiders", Jan 2). By contrast, environmental organisations and statutory bodies with a public grant many times bigger have removed only 5,600 stoats on Orkney since 2019 with no end in sight. The key difference appears to be that the coypu project knew it would end after ten years, whatever the result, and that if the trappers were successful they would get a bonus of up to three times their annual salary, declining as the ten-year deadline loomed. Perhaps it is time for the Public Accounts Committee to ensure taxpayers are still getting value for money from conservation projects.

Andrew Gilruth CEO, the Moorland Association

Sir, Crofters in the Highlands and Islands have the wits to wrestle a living from unpromising land and hostile seas. Why would Orcadians eradicate all their stoats when they get paid for killing them? It brings to mind that other ill-fated scheme: the bounty paid on grey squirrel tails.

Paul Shave Bo'ness, West Lothian

Roman riddle

Sir, Further to Jack Blackburn's article "Riddle of the Roman relic we can't get to grips with" (Jan 10), and Professor Alice Roberts's remarks in the television programme *Digging for Britain*, it seems to me that Lorena Hitchens's suggestion of revolving the dodecahedron around two fingers by means of the nodules seems at least half-right. All the holes in the sides of the item are clearly of different sizes. If a wooden ball were inserted inside, it would prove a decided challenge to see how many times one could complete a revolution without losing the ball. A simple precursor of the Rubik cube?

Nicholas de Mattos Shepperton, Surrey

Sir, I was delighted to read that another knobbly dodecahedron has been found, this time in Lincolnshire. It seems obvious to me that the Romans played pickleball.

Brian Mitchell Harpenden, Herts

Sir, The mystery of the dodecahedron found by archaeologists is easily solved: it is an early Romano-British model of the Covid-19 virus.

Jeremy Harris, Shipton-under-Wychwood, Oxon

Sir, The mysterious dodecahedron is surely no puzzle (letters, Jan 11; news, Jan 10) but an example of a Roman rangefinder, as described by Amelia Sporavigna in her paper "An Ancient Rangefinder for Teaching Surveying Methods" in *Engineering* (Vol 4, 2012).

Paul Silcocks Bamford, Derbyshire

Sir, I would hazard a guess that the "knobbly dodecahedron" is an early bowls "wood": the holes at the bottom are perfectly aligned for two fingers and a thumb. I suspect the skill lay in trying to ensure the "wood" landed with the biggest scoring hole facing upwards. It must have been more challenging with the knobs.

Sonia Swaine Ascot

Sir, The most convincing explanation for the function of the Roman dodecahedron is French knitting to produce tubular knitted products and gloves. This explains the balls that hold the yarn, the different-sized holes for different-diameter tubes and the multiple sets of these for making gloves. There are videos online showing the process with an actual dodecahedron. Just search for "Roman dodecahedron knitting".

Philip Blake Dingwall, Highland

Sir, It is obvious to me that the dodecahedron is a spanner for different sizes of wagon and chariot nuts and bolts.

Millius Palayiwa Oxford

Going nuts

Sir, I, too, decided to grease the metal bird-feeder pole to deter squirrels (Notebook, Janice Turner, Feb 8). My nearest solution to hand at the time was Deep Heat cream. The offending squirrel was very upset and surprised as he slid down the pole. He then hopped up and down as if on hot coals and rushed to stand in the nearby birdbath to give his feet some relief. He didn't return.

Ros White London NW4

Sir, Janice Turner (Notebook, Feb 8) could have further enjoyment by fixing a slinky (remember them?) round the bird-feeder pole. Watching the squirrels run up the pole and being hit on the head by the slinky provides many hours of enjoyment.

Phyllis Stuffins Altrincham, Greater Manchester

Sticky business

Sir, Regarding your report "Lyle's takes the sting out of golden syrup lion packaging" (Feb 20), about 50 years ago my boss, Lou Klein, was asked by Lyle's to redesign its golden syrup tin. It still makes me proud that Lou, head of graphic design at the Royal College of Art, refused on the grounds that it was already perfect.

Ruth Watson Sibton, Suffolk

Sir, We dipterists note the Lyle's golden syrup label change with regret, as we were not consulted (Feb 20). As specialist entomologists we can be pretty certain that the insects flying around the dead lion were not bees but *Eristalis* hoverflies, which breed in pools of corruption with larvae called rat-tailed maggots because they have long breathing tubes that enable them to inhale atmospheric air while submerged in rottenness. Adult *Eristalis* copy bees so well that Samson was deceived, as most people still are.

As for Lyle's taking the sting out of the label, not only do I agree with Ruth Watson (letter, Feb 21) on the merit of the original design but note that *Eristalis* hoverflies do not sting. As brilliant bee mimics, they don't need to.

Hugh Pennington Hoverfly collector for 50 years, Aberdeen

Right to roam

Sir, Alice Thomson says that urban children should learn more about their environment, food production and the countryside ("Someone has to pay for the right to roam", Mar 20). I have a dairy farm in Somerset and for the past four years, for ten minutes a week I connect via Zoom with a reception class from West Sussex to show the workings of my farm and to explain how milk is produced. It is an initiative called "Farmertime" and it is the highlight of my week.

Katrina Dunford Evercreech, Somerset

Sir, On a lovely walk recently we came across a "Private – No Entry" gateway in a wooded area leading to a small meadow. On a nearby tree was the bold notice: "No Trespassing. Violators will be shot. Survivors will be shot again." The rush to leave gave no time to enjoy the scenery.

Shayne Straker Southborough, Kent

Sir, We were walking the Thames Path when we passed several mansion-type houses overlooking the Thames (letter, Mar 21). On their back access gates to the river were the usual "Private – No Trespassing" notices. But one was particularly strict. It read: "No Stopping and Looking." We dutifully averted our eyes and scurried past.

Ruth Scott Abingdon, Oxon

Roaming pact

Sir, As a farmer I find it frustrating to see so much litter in the countryside (letters, Mar 19–21). This month a neighbour asked permission to walk their dog around our farm (colloquially it might be called "roaming"). My daughter came up with the idea that instead of any payment they should keep a certain area of road verges clear of litter. They have agreed to this deal. It should, if it works, mean that the roads leading up to our farm, farm shop and Pick Your Own are kept in a cleaner state. With some 13 million dogs, or dog owners, and 100,000 farmers in the UK there is the opportunity for this idea to be replicated. Our dog walkers will also keep an eye on "middle-class litter" such as posters for car boot sales, fêtes and cycle races, and other supposedly temporary signs that seem to remain for much longer than they should.

Richard Stanley Stanton St John, Oxon

Delicious dandelions

Sir, Jonathan Tulloch (Nature notes, Apr 19) rightly extols the virtues of dandelions but omits to add that they are a healthy, readily available food resource. Last week I picked nutritious nettle leaves but today it was dazzling dandelion flowers for my wife to bake and decorate delicious cakes for our weekend garden visitors.

Simon Brown Stevington, Beds

Battered weed

Sir, My two young grandsons happily harvest dandelion flowers from my garden (letter, Apr 22). Coated in a light batter, quickly fried, then sprinkled with icing sugar, these plants are delicious.

Helen Durell, Leigh-on-Sea, Essex

Sir, Dandelions also make a delicious salad in France, *salade de pissenlits*, known for its diuretic properties.

Robert Owen Poole

Fine and dandelion

Sir, Dandelion leaves are indeed a salad eaten in France (letter, Apr 23). But it is held that the leaves are best picked and eaten before the plant flowers. The leaves are considered too bitter afterwards.

Claire Richard Hurstpierpoint, W Sussex

Dandelion coffee

Sir, Simon Brown and Claire Richard have commented on the food value of dandelion leaves and flowers (Apr 22 & 24) but the roots of this plant can be also used to make a coffee substitute. In his 1972 book *Food for Free* Richard Mabey gives a recipe for dandelion coffee: "Dig up the roots in the autumn and scrub well (though do not peel). Dry thoroughly, preferably in the sun, then roast in an oven until brittle. Grind them coarsely and then use as ordinary coffee." I tried this successfully almost 50 years ago – despite my mother's repeated protestations at having dandelion roots in her kitchen.

Michael Laggan Newton of Balcanquhal, Perthshire

World
of
work

Knotty issue

Sir, I was interested to read Joe Spence, the master of Dulwich College, on the subject of the old school tie ("Ties that bind", letter, May 26). When I was at Cambridge in the 1960s my uncle, the author Eric Linklater, was engaged to address a college literary society on precisely that subject. He was brilliant and wickedly amusing and in the end he made a persuasive argument for his conclusion that the greatest practical use for the old school tie was to knot it round one's waist to hold one's trousers up.

Alastair Hume London N1

Tied up in knots

Sir, The main function of the old school tie (letters, May 26 & 30) was the knot in the shorter end to remind one the following morning to take in homework.

Geoffrey Silman London NW3

Sir, Apropos Alastair Hume's letter, I fear the weakness in the speech by his uncle, Eric Linklater, was that as one ages, one old school tie to hold up one's trousers is insufficient. I now need two.

Jeremy Gee Périgord, France

Cutting ties

Sir, Archbishop Runcie became increasingly tetchy as I interviewed him in the 1980s about the ordination of women. The TV camera switched off, the former Cambridge college dean pointed to my pink-striped tie (letters, May 26, 30 & 31) and said he really hadn't expected such a stiff encounter from an Emmanuel College man. I didn't go to Cambridge and the tie was from Marks & Spencer.

Bruce Parker BBC News 1967–2003,
Appleshaw, Hants

I'm not game

Sir, Gareth Wyn Jones suggests that spare game from shoots be donated to food banks (news, May 27). Brilliant idea, but who picks up the dental bill? Shot pellets lie deep and dastardly, as I know from experience. Tooth crowns don't come cheap.

Andrew Paulson Hucknall, Notts

Top of the range

Sir, Yesterday I passed a Tesla. Clearly the driver had range anxiety because he had a bicycle fixed to his roof rack.

Jack Cornforth Loughborough, Leics

Treading carefully

Sir, Drew Close's reflections on Mike Leadbetter's persuading Reform Club door people that his trainers were for medical reasons (letter, May 19) resonated strongly with me. As head teacher of a grammar school I enforced a strict uniform policy that forbade trainers. However, I had to relent on occasions when students produced medical notes written by my brother, a podiatrist.

Enda Cullen Armagh

Nocturnal widdling

Sir, Oliver Moody's article deserves an additional medical comment ("German men take a stand for sitting to spend a penny", May 22). Occasionally men who get out of bed in the middle of the night to pass urine may experience a sudden, severe drop in blood pressure causing loss of consciousness (micturition syncope), resulting in a fall and injury. Furthermore, if this condition is misdiagnosed the sufferer could be banned from driving. Hence, whatever a nation's diurnal male widdling conventions might be, mature men should certainly be advised to sit when passing urine in the night.

Dafydd Thomas Professor emeritus of clinical neuroscience, Imperial College

Sir, The Germans cannot claim bragging rights in the matter of being *Sitzpinklers*. As long ago as the 5th century BC the Greek historian Herodotus reported, with some astonishment and possibly even mild disgust, that in Egypt women urinated standing up, the men seated. Seated on what, he did not state, his point being that Egypt was a world turned upside down: they didn't just do things differently there.

Professor Paul Cartledge Clare College, Cambridge

Mocked medals

Sir, I have sympathy for Julie-Anne Fulford ("Veteran 'mocked by soldiers' for wearing her medals to Palace party", news, Jun 5). When I was ambassador in Yerevan my husband and I met a British barrister who was on a tour of the gardens of the South Caucasus. The gentleman established that I worked at the British embassy. "And what do you do in the embassy?" he asked. "Run it, on a good day," I replied with a smile and with what I thought was suitable modesty. "I thought the ambassador did that," he said. I then abandoned modesty. "She does," I said firmly. He did at least have the grace to blush. I hope Ms Fulford continues to wear her medals.

Thorda Abbott-Watt London W8

Weight of the law

Sir, It is not only advocates who snore ("Judge punishes lawyer for snoring", Jun 8). At the end of a week-long trial in Grimsby my closing submissions were (I thought) reaching new oratorical heights when the judge's eyes slowly closed and he started snoring. Speaking more loudly had no effect, nor did falling silent. I looked at my more experienced opponent, who simply laughed and muttered: "Your problem." Somewhat desperately, I picked up my weighty copy of *Chitty on Contracts* and let it fall on the desk with a loud bang. The judge jumped upright, blinked a few times and we carried on as if nothing had happened.

Guy Morpuss KC Farnham, Surrey

Silence in court

Sir, A juror fell asleep during my final speech (letter, Jun 9). I picked up an exhibit, a table leg used in the affray, and smashed it on to the desk. A large piece of the desk fell off, waking the juror and startling me. I wondered whether I would be charged with criminal damage, lost my train of thought and also the case. After that, I let them sleep on undisturbed.

Ronald Thwaites KC Esher, Surrey

Sir, A colleague of mine once complained to the judge that a juror was asleep during his speech. "You sent him to sleep so you can wake him up" was the judicial response.

Robert Woodcock KC Netherton, Northumberland

E-scooter alert

Sir, The idea of electric scooters having artificially generated noises is a good one, given that they tend to whizz perilously close to unsuspecting pedestrians ("Silent e-scooters are given a safer sound", Jun 27). Now we need to know if the Pavement Code – as opposed to the Highway Code – states whether the pedestrian's duty is to leap smartly sideways out of the way on hearing the sound. As a frequent pedestrian I would need to put in some practice with this manoeuvre, as I am in my eighties. I don't want to break the rules.

Christine Rogers Maidenhead, Berks

Don't stop me now

Sir, As I have to use a mobility scooter I understand the concern (letter, Jun 28) about the stealthy approach of e-scooters. I have managed to alleviate the problem by attaching a speaker to the buggy that is linked to my phone, and play a track from Queen so as to alert pedestrians of my approach.

Laurence Dillamore Cowes, Isle of Wight

RAF discrimination

Sir, How times have changed ("White airmen win RAF apology for discriminatory diversity drive", Jun 30). As a teenager in 1978 I went into the RAF recruitment centre in Northampton and expressed a desire to train as a pilot. I was given short shrift, with a curt: "Wrong plumbing, love." Instead I trained as a nurse.

Denise Greenspan Stoke Poges, Bucks

Digital AGMs

Sir, I strongly agree with your editorial (Jul 5) that M&S is wrong in not having an AGM in person. Before the lockdown I enjoyed attending AGMs to find out how the company was performing, and relished the engagement between the board and shareholders. The AGM was more than just about business: there was the social side, with coffee and cakes beforehand and lunch afterwards. We could mingle and chat with other shareholders and company workers. My favourite AGM was held in Cheapside, where we were entertained to a hot lunch with wine – we were also given presents of pencils, notepads and bottles of sparkling water. The result was that I have stayed loyal to that company, grateful for its first-class cuisine.

Canon Brian Stevenson West Peckham, Kent

Shareholder action

Sir, In 2018 our village postbox was vandalised and residents were left without one, necessitating a car journey to post a letter. My complaints to Royal Mail produced no result, so after eight months I wrote to the chairman to say that, as a shareholder, I would be turning up to the 2019 AGM (letter, Jul 6) to tackle him, which I did. He told me that a new postbox was being installed that very morning – and it was. I wonder how much longer it would have taken had I not turned up in person.

Teresa Sienkiewicz Lopen, Somerset

Alphabet soup

Sir, Although I agree with Hetan Shah (letter, Jul 5) on the importance of a broad education, I hope we can avoid any further acronyms. As a school governor, I have been given four A4 sheets of acronyms, beginning with ADD (attention deficit disorder) and ending with YOT (youth offending team). Most papers that I get to read introduce a new one and I will soon have five sheets. They make educational papers very time-consuming to read.

Lord Terrington London SW4

Leave well alone

Sir, Henry Wallop's demand that "holiday" is used on out-of-office messages rather than the ubiquitous "annual leave" exposes him as part of what my adult daughters call "the patriarchy" ("We all need a good holiday, but please give the snarky out-of-office emails a rest", business comment, Jul 28). Any woman knows that annual leave is very definitely not a holiday. Over the years I have taken "annual leave" days when childcare has fallen through, when children have been unwell, when domestic concerns have needed attention and to take elderly relatives to hospital appointments. And all that before we begin to unpick who is the "self" in the "self-catering" family holiday.

Ruth Godden Redhill, Surrey

Senior cycle couriers

Sir, As an economically inactive over-50, I note the advice from Mel Stride to get on my (Deliveroo) bike and work ("Get on your delivery bike, minister tells the over-50s", Aug 2). I suspect that most of my deliveries would be cold on arrival, as I was brought up to obey traffic light signals and to proceed only when they were green.

Paul Harvey York

Sir, I did get on my bike to work. I am over 70 and on my first outing fell off, scattering deliveries over the road. The majority of my expectant customers did not receive what they were hoping for. I decided to re-retire.

Charles Puxley Newbury, Berks

Age of experience

Sir, Trevor Phillips's reference to B&Q's hugely successful Macclesfield experiment in hiring over-50s staff in the 1990s (comment, Aug 28) reminded me of how it came about. Our agency, Bates Dorland, did B&Q's advertising, and its boss and I sat together among the 2,000-strong audience at the Retail Advertising Conference in Chicago listening to Home Depot recount how it did exactly that (we also pinched its idea of increasing store traffic at slow midweek trading times by offering a discount to OAPs on those days). What was particularly encouraging was the huge response received from local "senior" job applicants, and the research indicating that customers preferred to buy their wallpaper from staff who had clearly hung a roll or two, rather than being served by younger staff who obviously hadn't. If only politicians would take a leaf out of business's book, by trawling other countries' proven successes with "best of breed" ideas and copying them, instead of trying to reinvent the wheel, which so often results in costly failure.

Neil Kennedy Burnham on Crouch, Essex

Wheels of fortune

Sir, While reading Juliet Samuel's commentary on Germany's grim economic prospects ("Germany's travails are our problem too", Sep 14) I was reminded of similar articles in the early 1990s as the country faced considerable post-reunification headwinds. I had just moved to Bavaria and mentioned to my new boss that I might not have picked the best decade to pursue a career in Germany. I will never forget his deadpan response. "Yes, we Germans are faced with two major problems here: the recession and the long waiting list for a Mercedes." Thirty years later this still holds true.

Matthew Whittall Schönaich, Germany

Lack of face value

Sir, Those expressing concern about facial recognition leading to "dystopian surveillance" (letters, Sep 16) need not worry. My bank's app uses such technology and fails to recognise me more often than not and it has the advantage of knowing whom it is trying to identify.

Don Grocott Walton-on-Thames, Surrey

Computer says No

Sir, I share Don Grocott's frustration with facial recognition software (letter, Sep 18). My bank's system rarely works before the fourth or fifth attempt, if then. It fails completely in artificial light, and after a certain number of failed attempts it de-registers your phone, making it necessary to start again as a new customer.

And, in a Kafkaesque twist, you can only opt out of the facility by going through facial recognition first.

David Williams Great Waltham, Essex

Winking organist

Sir, I can understand David Williams's frustration with facial recognition software (letters, Sep 18 & 19) but as a church organist, when both hands and feet are occupied I rely on facial gestures to turn music pages on my laptop. If I twitch my mouth to the right it turns the page forward, and if to the left, backward. The same is supposed to be true of each eye but the software doesn't recognise my winking.

Laura Lockwood Seaton, Devon

Wartime allergy

Sir, I was interested to see your report from the Royal Pharmaceutical Society (Sep 29) that 90 per cent of people who believe they are allergic to penicillin are not. When I was a junior doctor in the 1970s we admitted an elderly man with a heart condition. He needed penicillin but "allergic to penicillin" was written all over his notes. My consultant asked me to talk to him to find more details. "It was in the trenches in the First World War, doctor," he told me. "They gave me penicillin and I had a terrible reaction."

I have no idea what he was given in the trenches but given that penicillin was not discovered until 1929 and not used until 1941 he was probably not allergic to penicillin.

Dr Peter Moore Marldon, Devon

On your feet

Sir, James Davies ("That's not a proper desk stretch! 7 ways to get fit at work", *Times2*, Oct 26) gives good advice on keeping active for those of us required to sit for long periods. One golden rule in our house is the self-imposed one that any weather forecast, whether on radio or TV, has to be listened to while one is standing up. Only mealtimes are excluded.

Jasper Stevens Southwick, W Sussex

Staying on

Sir, Robert Crampton is right about the joys of working on after retirement ("Many of my friends have retired. Here's why I won't be joining them", *Times2*, Oct 31). However, I have been anxious about the appraisals at work in the restaurant where I wash up. Fortunately the head chef has told me that, at 77 years old, I am to be let off. I suspect that the real reason is that finding someone else is too difficult.

John Longley Tisbury, Wilts

You may enter

Sir, This morning I read William Hague's excellent but startling article (Oct 31) on the threat posed by AI. This afternoon I was startled even more when I successfully logged on to my bank account using facial recognition software: it failed to spot my Lord of Darkness disguise, a dress rehearsal I had forgotten to remove before tonight's little Halloween visitors.

Charles Roberts Alsager, Cheshire

Sir, I have heard that it may be a wise precaution to include the word "please" in any online AI query, on the basis that when the computers take over, they will remember who was polite to them.

Chris Vollers Godalming, Surrey

Future is AI

Sir, You report that Elon Musk thinks that AI means nobody will have to work. When I did business studies in the late 1980s it was believed that the advent of computers would lead to a massive increase in leisure time. I was still waiting for this when I retired.

Liz Sutton Rudgwick, W Sussex

Sir, Elon Musk's prediction that "AI will outsmart us" comes almost exactly 50 years after a previous warning from an unlikely source: the rock band Emerson, Lake and Palmer (ELP). In the song *Karn Evil 9*, ELP portray a final battle between mankind and computers, which the computers win. It ends with a dialogue between the protagonists, with the computer having the last word: "I'm perfect. Are you?"

Alec Gallagher Potton, Beds

Call a doctor

Sir, I was interested in Dr Mark Porter's column about difficulty getting a GP appointment (*Times2*, Nov 14; letter, Nov 17). I was at my local surgery waiting for a blood test when a lady went up to the receptionist to make an appointment to see a doctor. She was told she could only do this by phone so took a step back from the desk, retrieved her phone from her pocket and dialled the surgery. I had to laugh at the absurd situation we find ourselves in, but I congratulate the lady highlighting the fact.

Alison Adams Shipston-on-Stour, Warks

AI hits the buffers

Sir, I spent 20 minutes this morning on the National Rail website trying to work out the right ticket to purchase to travel from Winchester to London on a specific mid-morning train and return on any train in the late afternoon. I then asked Bing AI. It replied in seconds that it couldn't work it out and that I should try the National Rail website. Thankfully Winchester station has a ticket office.

Dr Patrick Martin Winchester

Middle-class theft

Sir, Archie Norman, the chairman of Marks & Spencer, has the answer to the problem of pilfering in his hands ("Middle classes pilfer from self-checkouts, says M&S chief", Nov 21). If shoppers walk out without paying when scanners fail to register every item in their baskets, he should follow the example of Booths supermarkets and revert to staffed checkouts. M&S introduced self-service checkouts without any consultation with its customers and is paying the price.

John Bretherton West Wickham, Kent

Sir, The middle classes stealing from Marks & Spencer might think twice if there were any local newspapers left to report their crimes. Magistrates in Kent, where I first became a court reporter, often told shoplifters that exposure in the local newspaper was the greater part of the punishment.

Stephen Rayner Former reporter, *Chatham News*, Faversham, Kent

Sir, The correspondence about middle-class shoplifting has reminded me of an incident that occurred when I was a management trainee with Marks & Spencer. An elderly man was seen to be pocketing new socks, and his activity was drawn to my attention. Instead of creating a scene, I sidled up to him and surreptitiously removed the stolen socks. I have often wondered what he said on discovering the loss.

Roger Cookson London NW11

Remote GP consultations

Sir, Dr John Nathan (letter, Dec 1) stresses the importance of medical examination for GPs. As a young doctor doing a GP locum, I asked an elderly lady to go behind the screen and remove her clothes so I could examine her chest. "But I haven't come prepared to be examined," came the plaintive reply, but I persevered and in due course she left. On opening the door to ask for the next patient (no receptionists then), I heard the elderly lady's companion declare triumphantly: "I told you – he's an examining doctor!"

Professor Sir Nicholas Wright Kew, Surrey

Dig in for victory

Sir, Oliver Dowden advises us all to boost our personal resilience in the event of power cuts ("Don't panic but stock up on candles, batteries and torches", Dec 5). The over-60s have consistently warned the government about the increasing reliance on digital services, including the loss of high street banks, problems with parking apps and the removal of analogue telephone services, meaning that landlines do not work during power cuts. We have been generally ignored, but many of us do still keep the items he recommends in our homes for emergency use. However, we are most grateful to Mr Dowden for giving us all some very welcome Christmas present ideas for our children and grandchildren.

Caroline Tayler Nutley, E Sussex

Slim chance

Sir, As a GP for 30 years, my advice to my patients on how to lose weight always seemed to fall on deaf ears ("Economy pays heavy price as UK gets fatter", Dec 4). I thought desperate measures were needed and suggested to my partners that I reduce the size of the door into my surgery. Patients would then have to lose weight before they could see me again. This also fell on deaf ears, but sometimes you have to think outside the box.

Dr Chris Taylor Fernhurst, Surrey

Destination buffet

Sir, As a commuter for the past 30 years I could have told the Office of Road and Rail that buying food and drink at mainline stations such as London Liverpool Street has always been a rip-off ("Grab lunch at the station and it may cost 10% more", Dec 13). Whereas, at the other end of my commute, the legendary and independently run Manningtree Station Buffet's bacon bap and cuppa combo for £4.50 continues to sustain us weary travellers and our wallets.

Matthew Patten Manningtree, Essex

Teachers' presents

Sir, I never gave a thought to the cost of any present given me by a pupil ("Parents urged to give gifts for Miss a miss this Christmas", Dec 15). They were all of equal value, though I did have a favourite gift one year when I received a small four-herb dispenser: it introduced me to using herbs in cooking. A special present I was given at the end of teaching practice was from the girl I had found most troublesome. I think she must have raided her mum's cupboards, as among half a dozen items in a battered old Oxo tin were a pack of plasters and a card of sewing needles.

Gill Moss Poulton-le-Fylde, Lancs

Gifts of class

Sir, I agree with Gill Moss (letter, Dec 16) that teachers don't consider the monetary value of presents from their pupils. My most memorable and heartwarming present was given to me at a class Christmas party. It was a half-eaten sausage roll, wrapped in a screwed-up paper serviette. I suspect that the boy who gave it to me often went hungry and it must have been a great sacrifice. It was worth more to me than any expensive present.

Barbara Collins Nantwich, Cheshire

Sir, A teacher friend was amused to receive one Christmas an expensive bottle of port still sporting its security tag.

Cait Mercer Newark, Notts

What's in a name?

Sir, Monty Don might not enjoy being referred to as a horticulturist rather than a gardener (report, Jan 9) but my mum used to work in a school kitchen doing the washing-up and was really chuffed when she was referred to as the plate room attendant. She still got paid a pittance though.

Wendy Ross Leeds

Far horizon

Sir, Anyone familiar with the history of the Church of England should not be surprised that Paula Vennells, the former chief executive of the Post Office, almost became Bishop of London in 2017. In 1724, Lancelot Blackburne was appointed Archbishop of York despite having been a pirate in the Caribbean. From 1732 until his death in office in 1743, no ordinations whatsoever took place. Performing a rare confirmation at St Mary's Nottingham, he was ejected by the vicar, who took exception to the bored archbishop attempting to light a pipe and down a pint during the service. Definitely one for the ladies, Blackburne dug a tunnel from his deanery in Exeter to a nearby canon's house so that he could sport with his wife. As the satirist William Donaldson quipped: "His behaviour was seldom of the standard expected of a cleric; in fact it was seldom of the standard expected of a pirate."

The Right Rev David Wilbourne Honorary Assistant Bishop of York

Stand and deliver

Sir, Your headline "Sunak 'will not countenance' ending Saturday post delivery" (Jan 23) will have caused many a wry smile. In this part of Surrey we get one postal delivery a week – usually midweek – and for the rest of the week we queue up at the main sorting office to collect our letters. First- or second-class stamps make no difference, and for the second year in a row a high percentage of Christmas cards posted in December arrived here in mid-January.

Humfrey Malins Westcott, Surrey

Sir, Further to your report "Sunak 'will not countenance' ending Saturday post delivery" (Jan 23), the reason why Royal Mail must continue with Saturday deliveries is to ensure that all the post we should receive on Fridays is delivered only one day late, rather than three days late, as would otherwise be the case.

Dr Bob Sterritt East Grinstead, W Sussex

Ready, aim, fire

Sir, I am glad that Giles Coren looks back with fondness upon his school physics lessons ("Physics dull as dishwater? Not at 1980s Westminster", Notebook, Mar 5). My inspiration was Mr Smith at Cranbrook School in the 1980s. He illustrated the speed of sound to us with a Lee Enfield .303 in the outdoor rifle range. In my own lessons, I use air rifles and bows and arrows to illustrate many aspects of physics. Next Thursday is Pi day: we will be approximating Pi using the pattern produced by a shotgun. We'll go outside for that one.

Tim Sayers Head of Physics, Ardingly College, W Sussex

Fire in the sky

Sir, In the mid-1970s our physics teacher, Mr Lee, taught us the principle of electromagnetic induction (letter, Mar 7) by constructing an electric guitar fashioned from a length of broom handle, a square of plywood, an earpiece from his RAF flying helmet (as a pickup), a string purloined from the school Steinway and an old valve radio as an amplifier. When he plugged it in and plucked the string – only to reproduce, quite involuntarily, the opening three notes of Deep Purple's *Smoke on the Water* – the entire class gave him a round of applause. We loved him dearly.

Adrian Mallen East Boldon, Tyne & Wear

Work-life balance

Sir, Further to Will Lloyd's article on our changing attitude to work ("Forget coalface toil, Britain prefers to chill", Mar 4), as a retired person I am longing for people to go back to the office. My street used to be the sort of wasteland that Lloyd describes Canary Wharf as now. In the day I used to play loud music and stream noisy videos. People working at home now expect quiet. I think I will rent an office.

Tom Frost London SE10

Restorative justice

Sir, Further to your report "Courts in pubs 'would make them accessible'" (news, Apr 23), in the mid-1950s my father's band sergeant was pulled over in Northern Ireland for speeding in a Morris Minor. The court convened in a local bar and a fine was issued. "Court is closed," the magistrate declared. "The bar is now open." The fine paid for a handsome round.

Chris Crowcroft Penrith, Cumbria

Stairway to heaven

Sir, Further to your article on the benefit of taking the stairs ("A simple step to live longer – avoid taking the lift", Apr 27), as a fit 67-year-old I always choose the stairs and espouse the benefits to all who are prepared to listen. A sneaking part of me wonders, though, whether a careful analysis might reveal that the extra lifetime hours gained would turn out to have been spent climbing stairs.

Martyn Leadley, Corfe Mullen, Dorset

Food
and
drink

Flying fish

Sir, I had a small tin of tuna confiscated from my luggage at Gatwick last week: I was told it was because of the liquid around the tuna. It's difficult to know how that could be a threat. It takes me about ten minutes to open these tins. I wonder if Gatwick staff are replenishing their larder?

Susan Porter Burgess Hill, W Sussex

Easy as pie

Sir, A customs official at an American airport was going to confiscate my large pork pie (letter, May 29) so I broke it into chunks and those in the queue behind me enjoyed a nice snack.

June Keeble Storrington, West Sussex

Lost and found

Sir, What is missed by airports is as amazing as what is confiscated. I arrived in Madrid with two companions from Heathrow. When we stopped for a drink one friend, looking for his wallet, found two live 12-bore cartridges in an inside pocket of his shooting jacket. Half an hour later the other found his stalking knife, with a 5in blade, tucked under the base of his hand luggage bag. He had "lost" it several months before, and it hadn't been spotted on numerous trips in the meantime.

Rupert Godfrey Heytesbury, Wilts

Travel essentials

Sir, I am astonished Marmite does not feature in your list of holiday essentials ("Sunscreen, tinned beans and tea bags are all holiday essentials", May 24). My husband will not travel without it.

Judi Otter Wallace Barnet

Sir, On my last trip to Greece I arrived at Gatwick with a large jar of Marmite ("Travel essentials", letter, May 26) as a present for my sister, who lived there. It was confiscated on the grounds that it was a liquid. What an insult.

Imogen Thomas Saffron Walden, Essex

Beaver surprise

Sir, I wish Miriam Darlington good luck in her search for beavers (Nature notes, May 13). On holiday in the middle of France we were offered *le castor* for dinner, and a casserole of beaver was produced. It turned out that beavers were bred locally and were supplied frozen in the summer and fresh in the winter, with the pelt being used for slippers and gloves.

Katharine Minchin Easebourne, W Sussex

Simple pleasures

Sir, A fried jam sandwich is nothing new (News, Jul 14). It was in the culinary bible of my student years half a century ago: Katherine Whitehorn's *Cooking in a Bedsitter* (1961). It was the shortest recipe there: "Make jam sandwiches as if you were setting out for a picnic; and fry them till golden brown on both sides." Delicious.

Jenny Carr Edinburgh

One is fun

Sir, I have happily eaten alone in restaurants for years, accompanied by a book or Kindle, and in my experience nobody takes a blind bit of notice ("Dining solo moves up the menu at Michelin star restaurants", Jul 24). Any feelings of being regarded as a Billy-No-Mates are entirely in one's own head. I politely repel all boarders if I am approached by fellow diners "taking pity" on me. And on the only occasion when the service I received was discourteous, I found out on the local news the next morning that the restaurant had burnt down in the night. Karma!

Val Horsler Deal, Kent

Dinner for one

Sir, Further to your editorial "Dinner for One" (Jul 24; letter, Jul 25), until the start of this year I used to look with pity at those dining solo, with "There but for grace of God go I" springing to mind. Then it happened. My husband of 66 years died on New Year's Day after a fall. I found eating alone in our flat soul-destroying, given that only a few yards away was the local restaurant where we used to have our morning coffee. I quickly became a regular there at lunchtime and now go there every day. The staff come and chat and sometimes a friend will join me but I don't mind eating there alone as there is always a buzz, this being Hampstead. It has saved my sanity.

Angela Humphery London NW3

Going solo

Sir, Further to the letters on dining solo (Jul 25 & 26), one of my greatest pleasures is travelling alone on the train to London, a journey of two and a half hours of utter peace. Should anyone sit next to me and try to converse, my stock in trade response has always been "Je suis française. Je ne comprends pas" – until recently, when unfortunately my travelling companion proved to be French.

Anne Johnson-Rooks Thorncombe, Dorset

Sir, Emerging from my office in Bournemouth mid-evening, I decided to grab a bite in town rather than go home and cook a late meal. But three restaurants in a row declined to offer me a single table. "I have never been refused before," I complained when turned away a fourth time. "Madam, we are only seeking to spare you embarrassment," the proprietor said. "What lady would want to be seen dining alone on Valentine's Night?"

Marie Jackson South Barrow, Somerset

Tipping point

Sir, Further to Tony Turnbull's article "Confused about how much to tip? Perhaps I can be of service" (*Times2*, Aug 17), I am always surprised by the number of customers who insist that a jug of iced water should be free. I have to remind them that although the water is free I have to pay for the jug, the glass to drink it from, the cost and maintenance of the ice machine and the wages of the staff to serve it and clear up.

Ian Hudleston Passford House Hotel, Lymington, Hants

Here's a tip for you

Sir, Having experienced very indifferent attention in a New York hotel restaurant, the bill was placed before me with the comment that "service is not included". My response was that I had noticed. At that moment the server and I were divided by a common language.

Callum Beaton St Martin, Guernsey

Adieu, Le Gavroche

Sir, How sad to see the end of such a great institution ("Roux: I can't stand the heat so I'm shutting down Michelin restaurant", Aug 19). It was always such an intense personal experience from the warm welcome on arrival. The staff made it special. The Swiss soufflé was made to perfection. The best sommelier in town guided you through exciting new choices. Everyone was treated the same. Once as we walked down the stairs Michel Roux was sitting hard at work in his office late into the evening. We thanked him for the pure joy of eating there and he modestly seemed to be genuinely flattered.

Ian Elliott Belfast

Sir, Your leading article (Aug 19) notes that when Le Gavroche opened in 1967 Britain was in the culinary dark ages, with its restaurants famed for stodgily parochial menus. However, London already had other notable dining opportunities. To name but two, Veeraswamy, first established in 1926, offered a superb, genuinely Indian range of dishes – and continues to do so – and in Soho the Gay Hussar, which opened in 1953, provided an exciting introduction to Hungarian cuisine.

Martin French Cumnor, Oxon

More coffee, vicar?

Sir, As a vicar who can't stand the taste of tea ("Coffee overtakes tea as Britain's favourite drink", Aug 21), I welcome this recognition that my countercultural days might be coming to an end.

The Rev Canon Barbara Bilston Bacton, Suffolk

Holy orders

Sir, On funeral visits I always opt for tea over coffee (news, Aug 21; letter, Aug 22), partly because of the higher chance of drinkability but mainly because no bereaved family should be deprived of the fleeting pleasure of asking "More tea, vicar?"

The Rev John Lee York

Sir, I reckon Catholic priests do better than vicars (leading article, Aug 21). The one who visits us is given an open sandwich with smoked salmon and caviar and a cappuccino laced with Southern Comfort. He's usually happy to accept more.

Elizabeth Longrigg Oxford

Wine with an edge

Sir, There is little experimental about the use of plastic flat-sided wine bottles (news and leading article, Aug 28). In 2017 I received through the letterbox a flat-sided bottle of Chilean Sauvignon Blanc that I had ordered. The wine didn't last but the bottle has, as a souvenir, and it is virtually identical to the ones being used by the Wine Society. A price reduction might be wise if its idea is to catch on.

Malcolm Watson Ryde, Isle of Wight

Cuisine on campus

Sir, Tony Turnbull's article on student cooking (Weekend, Sep 23) reminded me of an undergraduate field trip in my first term. We were required to bring a packed lunch and the girl sitting next to me on the coach told me she had brought a boiled egg but did not know whether she had cooked it properly – was 45 minutes enough?

Teresa Sienkiewicz Lopen, Somerset

Food for thought

Sir, My late wife took a slightly different approach when we were students in Durham, preparing a picnic for us to eat on the banks of the River Wear below Finchale Priory. The hard-boiled egg I was offered (letter, Sep 25) was found not to have encountered water, boiling or otherwise.

David Mallett Richmond upon Thames

Sure as eggs

Sir, David Mallett had a nasty surprise with a raw egg at a picnic (letter, Sep 26). To avoid this unpleasant episode I always spin the egg on a flat surface. If cooked it will spin, if raw it will not.

John Shaw Tavistock, Devon

Boiled alive

Sir, I cook lobsters but would never boil them alive and was unpleasantly surprised to learn that this barbaric practice still continues ("Animal charity threatens action over lobster boiling", Sep 25). A fishmonger advised me to pop it in the freezer to render it comatose, then use a sharp knife at the back of its head to kill it quickly – a method also recommended by Keith Floyd.

Wendy Attridge Stroud, Glos

Drowning a lobster

Sir, Although lobster is one of my favourite meats my palate used to be dulled by the thought of the creatures being boiled alive (letters, Sep 25 & 26). This problem was solved for me years ago by an old Scottish lobster fisherman in the village of Crail. He taught me to kill the lobster by immersing it in hand-hot water for at least five minutes, which invariably left them unconscious so that they did not react when put into boiling water. I think this was humane because the water was never hotter than your own hand could stand. He called the method "drowning" the lobster.

Roger Hayes Llangadog, Carmarthenshire

Meaty vegetarians

Sir, I was amazed to read that those who "are vegetarian most or some of the time" are noted by the Vegetarian Society as one of their number, and that "approximately 48 to 64 per cent of self-identified vegetarians report consuming fish, poultry and/or red meat" ("Genes may hold key to staying meat-free", news, Oct 5). It would seem that, on this basis, I – a beef farmer and enthusiastic carnivore who enjoys a jam sandwich in the afternoon – should join the society as soon as possible.

Charlie Flindt Hinton Ampner, Hants

Addictive foods

Sir, For those who are wondering how to minimise their consumption of ultra-processed foods ("Ultra-processed foods 'addictive'", news, Oct 10), I recommend my three rules for healthy eating, devised in about 2005 to assist the GPs and others I was working with as a pharmacist interested in improving public health: if it comes in a shiny packet, or if it is nationally advertised, or if you think it may have come from a nozzle in a factory, don't make it a major part of your diet.

Dr Brian Curwain Lymington, Hants

Avoiding bad food

Sir, Dr Brian Curwain (letter, Oct 11) suggests a simple rule for avoiding highly processed food. Here is another: if it takes more than 20 seconds to read the list of ingredients, don't buy it. Unless of course it is minestrone soup.

Lesley Beckett Reading

Sir, My mother maintained, back in the 1970s, that you should never eat anything that you couldn't pronounce or that had emulsifiers in the list of ingredients. I still follow this today.

Yvonne Bailey Christian Malford, Wilts

Curly crusts

Sir, Matthew Parris reports that Witney police have been criticised for throwing their sandwich crusts into the gutter (Notebook, Oct 11). My mother brought me up to believe that eating my crusts would give me curly hair. That there was no medical basis for this became evident as I grew up. Similarly, experiments have shown that eating bread crusts does not improve one's whistling.

Geoff Brownlee Hornby, N Yorks

French fast food

Sir, With regard to the increasing prevalence of ready meals in French restaurants (report, Oct 24) we have noticed the tendency of restaurants in the department of Aude to have a sign outside saying, in effect, that they go to market, then peel, chop and generally slave away, cooking everything from scratch. The identical nature of these signs plants the seeds of doubt.

Sue Pheasey Amberley, W Sussex

Tinned perfection

Sir, French restaurants are not the only ones shunning fresh food (letter, Oct 25). On a recent visit to Piemonte, which prides itself on its fresh truffles, we were amused to find anchovies presented artistically on a plate in their tin. The lid and ring pull were at a jaunty angle and the accompanying garnish was stylishly Italian.

Dr Fiona Cornish Cambridge

Red or white?

Sir, We are regularly invited to dinner parties and, as ever, face the quandary of whether to bring a bottle of white or red, or indeed something sparkling. My feeling is that women generally prefer white, and men red, but other than bringing one of each, how is one to decide? I would greatly value other readers' opinions on this delicate matter of etiquette.

Anna Field Norwich

The perfect present

Sir, Further to Anna Field's dilemma of whether to take a bottle of red or white wine to a dinner party (letter, Oct 27), a good host will already have the red breathing or the white chilling but would welcome a chilled rosé as an aperitif and to break the ice.

Patricia Langtry Northwood, Middx

Sir, Why take wine to a dinner party? Keep bees – and take honey. It's always welcome.

Christopher Murray Barford St Michael, Oxon

Sir, I've found that a jar of my homemade whisky marmalade always hits the spot.

Anne Dove Swansea

Sir, Anna Field should leave the choice of wine to her hosts. A small gift, perhaps a copy of *Sir, The Year in Letters*, would provide lasting memories of an enjoyable evening. Who knows, her letter might even feature in its pages next year.

Callum Beaton St Martin, Guernsey

Sir, Your host will surely have provided wine already. My guests are bidden to bring the biggest box of Maltesers they can find, a large bar of Cadbury's Dairy Milk and Smarties for the grandchildren.

Barry Hyman Bushey Heath, Herts

Sir, I couldn't help wondering whether the letter from Anna Field on the etiquette of which wine she should bring to a dinner party had got lost in the post somewhere around 1975.

Ba Keeler Whitstable, Kent

Sir, This summer a guest surprised and delighted me with a fine bottle of extra virgin olive oil, which has contributed to the content of several subsequent dinner parties.

Mary Soutar Whitstable, Kent

Sir, I take golf balls to a dinner party. If my host or hostess doesn't play there is always someone there who does, so they can be passed on to that somewhat surprised fellow guest.

Charles Puxley Easton, Berks

Sir, Some years ago we helped a friend, who was married to a doctor in Pakistan, to wind up her father's affairs when he passed away. Months later, when they visited the

UK, we invited them for dinner. We didn't expect a bottle of wine but neither did we expect the rolled-up carpet he carried in over his shoulder, or the box of mangos.

Beryl Whyatt Welwyn Garden City

Sir, One of my best presents from a guest coming to dinner was six sacks of manure, carried to the bottom of the garden. He knew the way to a woman gardener's heart.

Helen Comrie North Curry, Somerset

Sir, A box of earthworms has proved an acceptable dinner party gift round here – for composting rather than consumption. Our acid soil supports very few but we have a thriving colony in our vegetable compost bin, descendants of some we brought with us from the south more than 20 years ago.

Hilary Brown Gairloch, Wester Ross

Sir, Shortly after I had installed a pond in my garden a dinner party guest presented me with the gift of a bucket of water from his pond. "It's full of newts" was his reply to my somewhat surprised reaction. After 15 years his present is still giving pleasure.

Dr Ronald Watson Slinfold, W Sussex

Spiky puzzle

Sir, I was dismayed by Sainsbury's proposal to sell crownless pineapples ("Off with their heads: pineapples lose crown", Nov 1). How will we play our much-loved family game of "guess the number of leaves on the pineapple" on Boxing Day?

Jill Alexander London SE21

Premier pineapple

Sir, For years now each person sitting around our Christmas dinner table has tried to guess how many leaves there are on the crown of the pineapple (letter, Nov 3). With mounting suspense, the leaves are removed one by one: the total may often exceed 100. The proud winner then holds the title of "*Mastermind* pineapple" for the following year.

Rosalind Barney Wymeswold, Leics

Infallible test

Sir, Pulling a leaf from the top of a pineapple (letters, Nov 3 & 4) is the best test for ripeness that there is. How is one to do this if there are no leaves?

Jane Lambourne Longton, Lancs

Side of greatness

Sir, What was Hannah Evans thinking of, calling cauliflower cheese "a side" (*Magazine*, Nov 4)? In a tasty white sauce it admittedly makes an accompanying vegetable with the roast but in a good cheese sauce with, perhaps, the addition of cheese and breadcrumbs on the top for the crunch it is a proper meal. If you really want to take it to another level add hard-boiled eggs and boiled potatoes: a truly vegetarian dish.

Katharine Minchin Easebourne, W Sussex

Sweet success

Sir, I applaud any effort to improve health and happiness ("The secret of my long life: I may be 102 but I have a ten-year plan", Nov 18). I was especially pleased last week when my activity tracker recorded "goal" for vigorously hand-beating home-made fudge. Wellbeing achieved on every level.

Jane Park-Weir Ellisfield, Hants

Microwaved steak

Sir, Even the best-quality steak can be rendered tough and unappealing when microwaved ("A rare suggestion: microwaved steak", Nov 21). Instead, get a ribeye steak from one of the five best beef breeds (all Scottish) – longhorn, shorthorn, Angus, Galloway or Highland – rub it with black pepper and cook it in a very hot pan containing a tablespoon of extra virgin olive oil. Sear the steak on both sides, seasoning with salt as it cooks, then three minutes in a hot oven. Rest the steak for five to ten minutes before serving. Delicious, simple and straightforward.

Claire Macdonald Kinloch Lodge, Isle of Skye

Ultimate fusion

Sir, While culinary fundamentalists may splutter about M&S's new line of "Spanish Chorizo Paella Croquetas" ("One paella of a mistake: M&S mixed dish panned", news, Nov 28), I wonder what they would make of the fine dish of Tandoori Haggis Masala that I once spotted on the menu of a Scottish Indian restaurant. There is a fine line between cultural appropriation and inspired fusion.

Andy Davey Peebles, Scottish Borders

Mine's a pint

Sir, Your piece on the best shape of glass for champagne omits another option ("Forgo flutes for our fizz, say French", Dec 5). My late mother, who worked at a wine bar in The Strand in the 1920s, described City businessmen consuming champagne from silver mugs on their way to work. I have my grandfather's silver pint mug, which is my choice container for bubbly. It has tapered sides to help retain the aroma and bubbles, and the silver helps to keep the contents suitably cool. I also emulate those City gents on Christmas Day by having a pint of champers at breakfast, after which I cruise through the morning six inches above the ground.

Dick Godfrey Newcastle upon Tyne

Bubbles of elation

Sir, While part-admiring and part-reproaching Dick Godfrey for drinking a pint of champagne at breakfast on Christmas Day (letter, Dec 6), I cannot but wonder whether his cruising height of six inches is in the upright or horizontal position.

Dr Jeremy Auchincloss Elgin, Moray

Make it a double

Sir, Further to the discussion about champagne at breakfast, in the Sixties Victor Lanson of the Lanson champagne house told me that a magnum – the equivalent of two bottles – was the appropriate size bottle for a gentleman breakfasting alone.

Robin McLaren Berkhamsted, Herts

Corking idea

Sir, Apropos of safety warnings on opening a champagne bottle ("50mph corks could leave you blind sober", Dec 21), I always understood that it should be carried out in a controlled way such as to evoke the sound of a dowager duchess breaking wind.

Dawn Philipps Great Missenden, Bucks

Pull the other one

Sir, To avoid the dangers of high-velocity champagne corks, grasp the cork firmly and gently rotate the bottle. Less spectacular but far safer.

Nick Murray Luton

Sir, When I open a champagne bottle, the cork does not move. It goes into the vice and I carefully remove the bottle.

Jeffery Wear, C Eng Broadstone, Dorset

Fit for an Iron Lady

Sir, Dominic Sandbrook ("A PM's diet is rarely just about the food", Feb 3) is wrong in thinking that Margaret Thatcher's "mystery starter" – a mixture of Philadelphia cheese, curry powder and a tin of undiluted beef consommé – is a punishment. It is in fact delicious. It was a regular dish of mine in the Eighties and is called Snaffles mousse. Thank you for reminding me of it.

Deborah Chalmers Tring, Herts

Sir, I was heartened to read Deborah Chalmers's letter (Feb 5) about Snaffles mousse. At a dinner party some years ago my wife served this mousse, only for it to be rejected by all the guests. It has never been served again. Sadly, it was my favourite.

Antony Haslam Wark-on Tyne, Northumberland

Ultimate toastie

Sir, Further to your report "French gourmets go gooey for a new delicacy: cheese toasties" (Feb 28), my favourite toastie is in Hannah Glasse's *The Art of Cookery Made Plain and Easy* published in 1747. Melt cheese with white wine, butter and mustard. Toast bread, moisten it with red wine, cover with the cheese mixture and brown it – the recipe says with a hot shovel but an ordinary grill will do. It is delicious.

Julian Dussek Plaxtol, Kent

Bite-sized flavour

Sir, Last summer I was picking at a bowl of cherries while reading *The Times* when I realised that they tasted decidedly more delicious than usual, if a little crunchy. Upon investigation I realised that an army of ants had got there first. Fortunately I am not easily put off my food and simply rinsed them off and carried on. But I can verify that "common black ants have a sour, vinegary taste" ("What tastes of caramel and nuts? My new favourite ant", Mar 18). They certainly complemented my rather bland cherries.

Viv Mercer Southport, Merseyside

Wine for runners

Sir, The drinking of wine during a marathon began before 1924 ("How red wine fuelled 1924 Olympians", Apr 19). William Sherring, winner of the 1906 Athens marathon, recommended a little Mariani wine as a good stimulant. However, Charles Hefferon, who was in the lead of the 1908 race, admitted that two miles from the finish he accepted a glass of champagne that gave him cramp and he ended up coming second behind Johnny Hayes (who gargled with brandy during the race). Also, participants in the Ancient Olympics took potions that almost certainly contained alcohol.

Nigel à Brassard Sports historian, London SW7

Marathon session

Sir, It is not only wine that can help runners (letter, Apr 22). On the eve of the 1986 Wolverhampton marathon I drank four pints of Timothy Taylor's Landlord beer. Although not feeling that great on the start line, I ran a personal best of 2 hours 39 minutes and then drank another four pints of Landlord straight after.

Gary Rawlinson Burbage, Wilts

26-mile pub crawl

Sir, My brothers and I, now all in our late 50s and early 60s, occasionally run a marathon between six pubs for fun (letters, Apr 22 & 23). We call it El Diablo (six pints, six hours and six runners for the first one). Many of our children and their spouses join in, and drinks other than beer (which is great for both hydration and carb replenishment) are now permitted. Beer remains very popular, though I favour whisky and noticed quite a lot of gin and tonic among the next generation, but no wine at all until the post-race dinner.

Mike Tod Lincoln

Fizzing with energy

Sir, On my first attempt at a marathon, in the inaugural London Marathon in 1981, I was unaware of hydration needs and about halfway round, somewhere in the Isle of Dogs, I dived into a pub for some refreshment (letters, Apr 22–24). A local at the bar insisted that I have, at his expense, a pint of Buck's Fizz, which I downed in one. I finished strongly in the first half of the field.

John Clachan Westcott, Surrey